Pen Pictures

by

Beverly Carradine

First Fruits Press
Wilmore, Kentucky
c2015

Pen Pictures, by Beverly Carradine

First Fruits Press, ©2015
Previously published by the Pentecostal Herald Press, 1901, © 1900.

ISBN: 9781621714330 (print), 9781621714347 (digital), 9781621714354 (kindle)

Digital version at http://place.asburyseminary.edu/firstfruitsheritagematerial/114/

First Fruits Press
B.L. Fisher Library
Asbury Theological Seminary
204 N. Lexington Ave.
Wilmore, KY 40390
http://place.asburyseminary.edu/firstfruits

Carradine, Beverly, 1848-1931

Pen Pictures / by Beverly Carradine.
342 pages ; 21 cm.
Wilmore, Ky. : First Fruits Press, ©2015.
Reprint. Previously published: Louisville, KY : Pentecostal Herald Press, 1901, © 1900.
ISBN: 9781621714330 (pbk.)
1. Christian fiction. I. Title.

PS3505.A7712 P4 2015

Cover design by Kelli Dierdorf

asburyseminary.edu
800.2ASBURY
204 North Lexington Avenue
Wilmore, Kentucky 40390

First Fruits
THE ACADEMIC OPEN PRESS OF ASBURY SEMINARY

First Fruits Press
The Academic Open Press of Asbury Theological Seminary
204 N. Lexington Ave., Wilmore, KY 40390
859-858-2236
first.fruits@asburyseminary.edu
asbury.to/firstfruits

REV. B. CARRADINE, D.D.

PEN PICTURES,

BY

BEVERLY CARRADINE,

AUTHOR OF

"Pastoral Sketches," "A Journey to Palestine,"
"The Old Man," etc., etc.

◆◆◆◆◆◆◆◆

PENTECOSTAL HERALD PRESS
LOUISVILLE, KY.

1

PREFACE.

The stories and sketches composing "Pen Pictures" I have written as I did "Pastoral Sketches" and "A Journey to Palestine," with a view to interest, while benefiting the head and heart of the reader. In my judgment it is my best literarv work. At the same time there is scarcely a chapter but has a moral or religious point, and so presented as to abide in the memory and affect the life. Flash-light revelations of character, the law of conscience, the power of human influence, kindness to animals, consideration for children, pity for the unfortunate, and many other lessons of life are taught in this volume. A number of the chapters are descriptive of actual adventures in the life of the writer; but still in the narrative an underlying purpose is felt, and a lasting moral or spiritual truth conveyed. Some people need to have a good laugh, some crave the luxury of tears, and others ought to pray. We doubt not that these three classes will find all they want in the pages of this volume.

THE AUTHOR.

TABLE OF CONTENTS.

PEN PICTURES.

I.

A SWAMP ADVENTURE.

THE Yazoo Delta is located in the northwestern part of the State of Mississippi. Its natural boundary lines are the Mississippi River on the west, and the Yazoo, running in a northeasterly direction, on the east. Starting from a point below Vicksburg, and skirting the right bank of the Yazoo River are the Walnut Hills. Like the river, they go in a diagonal direction across the north-central part of the State. Between these hills and the Mississippi River, fifty to seventy-five miles to the west, stretches the famous Yazoo Swamp. At distances of ten and fifteen miles, and almost in parallel lines, a number of creeks and small rivers flow southward across this swamp country and empty into the Yazoo at different points above where it joins the Father of Waters. These smaller streams are Silver Creek, Deer Creek, the Little Sunflower and Big Sunflower Rivers. The design, if traced on a piece of paper, would look somewhat like a harp, the Mississippi being the upright beam, the Yazoo the diverging column, and the streams just mentioned the strings.

On the banks of the four lesser streams are found many of the plantations which made the South famous. But after leaving these mile-wide cultivated strips the traveler would have to traverse a veritable jungle until he came to another creek, lake or river, with its cultivated region, beyond which would stretch another howling wilderness, and so on through these alternating plantation belts, and great dismal swamps, until at last one stood on the banks of the King of Rivers.

The swamp we are speaking of in this chapter was the first in order, and lay between the Walnut Hills and the Yazoo River. It varied from five to ten miles in width and was over fifty miles long. It was a gloomy stretch of shadowy woods, cypress and canebrakes and rustling palmettos. The cypress trees trailed from their branches long banners of gray moss, while from the tops of other monarchs of the forest, great vines fifty feet and more in length, and thick as a human limb, fell earthward, and looked in their natural twists and convolutions like immense anacondas and boa-constrictors, ready and waiting for their prey.

On the ground was a thick, brown carpet of leaves which had been steadily forming for many years. The trunks of prostrate trees overthrown by storms, or fallen through decay, were spotted with gray and white as by a leprous touch. The light that filtered through the thick foliage above, was of a misty, veiled order, which served to make the shadowy vistas all the more spectral, and prepared the thumping heart for a greater leap at the appearance, now not unexpected, of some uncanny thing or being in a neighboring or remote opening of the woods.

To stand alone, even at mid-day, in the midst of this swamp was an experience never to be forgotten. The sky would be almost entirely shut out by the interwoven branches and leaves overhead. The only sounds to be heard was the occasional fall of an acorn, the tap of a woodpecker, the scream of a blue jay, or cry of some strange bird hidden away in thicket or lagoon. When these were not noticed, then the listener became conscious of a sound that, no matter how often heard, always sent the blood tingling through the body and an awestruck feeling to the soul. It was the sigh of the woods ! the voice of the forest itself. It would steal upon the ear a faint, far off murmur ;

rise to a soft, plaintive wail for minutes, and then
die away into a silence, which was as affecting as
the sound itself. Sometimes the sigh would be
kept up unbrokenly for minutes before it would
cease its complaint, and sink to rest in some remote depths of the wilderness. The writer never
stood near the edge of this swamp, entered into its
borders, or rode through its extent, without hearing this peculiar melancholy sound. It seemed to
be a lament over something in itself, and a proph-
ecy of trouble. It might well have stood for the
sorrowful things which had taken place within its
own dark boundaries.

Some gruesome occurrences had transpired in
past years along its bayous and in its depths which
made a number reluctant to go alone through it in the
day and positively refuse to journey by night. There
had been several murders or suicides, none knew
which, and there was no way of finding out, as the
woods never told its secrets, but kept on sighing.
There had been a number of drownings in branch,
slough, and bayou. One in particular comes back
to the mind. Two negro men had been sent to
drive a yoke of oxen across the swamp to the
river. There had been a heavy rain, which
had swollen a bayou and caused it to overflow its

banks; the negroes, thinking they could wade across, drove the oxen into the water, and saw them immediately swept off their feet, and, hampered by the yoke, drown, and float away in the current. The two men swam to a tree, and, climbing up to a fork, sat there for hours, calling in vain for help. At last, in the dusk of the evening, one of them, despairing of assistance, leaped from the tree with the intention of swimming to the shore, but, to the horror of his comrade, after making a few efforts, sank before his eyes. The other remained on his lonely perch through the night, shouting at intervals, but answered only by hooting owls. Late next day he was rescued by a passing hunter, more dead than alive.

There were numerous instances like this, most of them connected with a certain bayou, which rising in the hills, stole through the swamp with a serpentine course, and winding around a part of the western edge of the woods, necessitated a crossing by ford or ferry in order to reach the plantations beyond. This stream had a number of times paid tribute to the Yazoo River in the shape of dead bodies of men, who, bewildered in the night, had attempted to cross in the wrong place, and sinking in the mud, or becoming entangled in the

vines, were finally swallowed up and afterwards
borne away by the yellow tide.

Owing to the faint trails through the swamp,
and their frequent crossing of one another, it was
difficult for a person to get through even in the
day time ; while to attempt the task at night meant
perfect failure to any one except those most familiar with the paths of the forest. Even they, on
dark nights, would be puzzled and have to wait
for the moon to rise or the day to break in order
to pursue their journey. Hence the cries of noc-
turnal birds and prowling animals were not the
only sounds that proceeded from the swamp after
nightfall. Oftentimes from its dark depths came
the shout or cry of a belated and lost traveler, which
would be succeeded and swallowed up later by the
distant hooting of owls.

A lady, well known to the writer, lived, during
the Civil War, on the western edge of this swamp,
her plantation being skirted by the woods. Her
dwelling was a quarter of a mile from the forest,
and there were nights when she said she could hear
these calls and cries of lost travelers. There was
no one whom she could dispatch to their relief, as
the negroes had been driven or enticed away by
the Federal soldiers ; so the shouts would die away

as the man wandered further off, and nothing would be heard save the cry of some distant night bird. She said, " the melancholy impressions of those nights would never be effaced."

The swamp had a population peculiarly its own ; a number of deer, a few bear, panthers and cata- mounts, some wild turkeys and every kind of owl and variety of bird. It had also its turtles, sleep- ing on sunlit logs, or falling with a "plunk" into the green sloughs at the snapping of a twig ; and snakes coiled up and looking like a bunch of autumn leaves, or dragging their spotted length across the trail before you. In addition to these natural deni- zens, were the lost travelers of whom I have spoken, and during the war a band of men who were de- serters from the Confederate ranks, or flying from draft and conscription, took to this tangled wilder- ness for refuge, and there, building huts of palmetto, and feeding on fish, turkey, the flesh of the wild hog and such other things as they could silently snare or entrap, they kept a watchful eye out for government officers, and would disappear like a flash in a cane-brake where it would have taken an army to find them.

On one occasion, the writer went with a num- ber of friends on a deer hunt. Two of the party

were Confederate officers home on furlough. We
had penetrated deep into the swamp and were
swiftly following the dogs, whose cry was growing fainter and fainter in the distance as they followed the game. Something had happened to make
the deer avoid the "stand," and, forsaking the
usual run on the ridge, go deep into the forest.
One of the officers and the writer, then a lad, found
themselves together galloping at as great speed
after the pack of receding hounds as the cane, palmetto and jungle-like woods would allow, when
suddenly there stood before us, leaning on his gun,
and not twenty yards away, a deserter. When he
glanced up and saw the uniformed man by my side,
his astonishment was as great as his instantaneous
flight was rapid. The soldier gave a great outcry
and spurred his horse to a swift pursuit. How the
man escaped us has ever been a mystery. The next
time we saw him he was fully an hundred yards
away in the middle of a cypress slough leaping
from log to log and going where we could not possibly follow. He seemed to thoroughly know his
ground, or rather lack of ground, and had we attempted to cross as he did the result would have
been death to the horses and certain disaster to ourselves. We had one more distant glimpse of him

through an opening of the trees. He had crossed
the quagmire and stood for a moment looking back
at us, when, with a bound, he plunged into a cane-
brake and disappeared.

As a boy of thirteen, I first saw this swamp,
heard it sigh, felt its strange, sorrowful presence,
and stood in fear and awe of its secrets, its known
and unknown history.

I recall standing just outside my mother's plantation, close to the border of the forest, and peer-
ing into its far-away depths, curiously, wistfully,
and yet fearfully. I wanted to go in, but the dark
shadows, gloomy vistas and that solemn sigh kept
me back.

A few months later I had penetrated the woods
a half mile alone and after that, a mile. At fourteen, gun in hand, I found myself two miles deep
in the swamp, on the banks of a cypress-brake,
beyond which the forest stretched away with even
darker depths, and more melancholy sounds. Hunters told me of other brakes and bayous beyond,
where wild game abounded and Indians came in
the fall to hunt.

Of course, I went deeper after that, until I reached
the heart of the forest, and knew that miles of dense
woodland stretched on every side of me. To this

day I recall the lonely scene, the dark vistas of the woods, the moss-grown and mouldering logs, the matted and knotted vines falling from lofty limbs to the ground and running like suspension bridges from tree to tree. I still remember the awful stillness of the hour and place, broken only at intervals by the weird cry of the rain-crow on some tree top, the hoarse boom of a frog from a brake, or that mournful sigh coming up from invisible and unknown regions of the forest.

At fifteen I knew well some of the trails across the swamp, and one day, while on horseback, I met in its very center a carriage with a negro driver on the box and three ladies inside, all looking bewildered, evidently lost, and not knowing what to do. It was a beautiful October afternoon and the autumn leaves were falling silently like a golden rain through the woods. To this day I recall the anxious face of the driver and the troubled countenances of the lady and her two handsome, dark-eyed daughters.

Taught by my mother to be always gallant and polite to ladies, I offered my services to guide the distressed group out of the swamp, yet I must admit that the two pair of dark eyes turned appealingly to me, would have been sufficient to prevent me from proving recreant to my early training. By this act of courtesy, however, I was led a number of miles directly away from home, and it was already late in the afternoon. There was a volley of fervent thanks from the carriage window :

"Oh, you are so kind."

"How can we sufficiently thank you," etc., etc.

In the midst of it all I headed the procession, with leaves falling upon us, or rustling under the horses' feet, and led the way to the farther side of the swamp.

The ladies were now able for the first time to note the gold and crimson beauty of the woods, apart from the terror of its shadowy depths and solemn moan, which rose and fell like a requiem.

When I left the party an hour later, in sight of the open fields and blue hills beyond, fervent expressions of gratitude from the inmates of the carriage were again repeated ; but insisting I had done nothing but what gave me pleasure, I galloped back in the forest, leaving the negro driver my life-long friend, and saying with every tooth revealed :

"I's sho glad we done meet you dis day."

And yet only a few months after this occurrence I lost my way after nightfall in the heart of this same forest, and had to wait for hours at the foot of a tree until moonrise in order to find the road. I shall never forget the convention the owls held over the affair, nor the blood-curdling "hoo-hoos" and "hah-hahs" of which they freely delivered themselves. As to the "who," I knew well enough the troubled individual ; and as to the laughter over his predicament, I felt he might well have been spared. If they had only known how the lost lad had been forced into their company, and was only too anxious to find his way back to civilization, they surely would have had pity on his ears and fears during that long night.

I was twenty-two years of age when one night the following occurrence took place in this memorable swamp.

At the time, I was associated in business with a gentleman who was planting and merchandising together, having a couple of plantations which lay at the foot of the hills, and on the eastern line of the swamp. Learning late one night that this friend was to be robbed of a certain number of cotton bales, then lying at one of the Yazoo River landings, I determined to give him warning at once. Had I waited until next day it would have been too late. I was at the time on the western edge of the swamp. It was then nine o'clock, and the wide, black, sighing forest lay between me and the man I desired to warn.

I never hesitated, however, but, flinging myself on a fleet, bay mare, soon crossed the plantation and entered the woods. It was quite dark, and I had to trust much to the horse, while urging her into a gallop whenever the road and a few star-lighted spaces made it possible. I had progressed swiftly, and well, and was just in the center of the swamp, when, glancing to the right, where an old road had made a semicircular bend about a fallen tree, I saw, twenty feet away, what seemed to be a gigantic man, with a dark face, and hair and beard white as snow. There was a sudden leap of the heart into the throat, the horse gave a snort and swerved aside ; but being in a hurry, and having no desire anyhow to stop and examine into such a strange and supernatural looking spectacle, at such an hour and in such a place, I swept on, leaving the real or imaginary thing behind, and in due time came out into the midst of broad corn and cotton fields, with the stars shining softly and reassuringly upon me, and the lights of the house I was approaching, twinkling in the distance.

I found that the gentleman had retired, but was

reading in bed. After telling him why I had taken the long night ride, and he had decided as to his course of action, I bade him good-night and prepared to return, steadily refusing his invitation to remain. Just as I was about to open the door, he called out, saying :

"Be careful as you go through the swamp tonight. The darkies say there is a crazy negro loose in the woods, as big as a giant and his hair as white as cotton."

Instantly I recalled the vision I had beheld in the forest, and told my friend I had already seen the crazy man.

With another warning from him to "look out," I closed the door, and mounting my horse, now fresh again from a half hour's rest, was soon cantering across the fields.

A silver haze stretched in lines or hung in banks over the quiet landscape. The glittering constellation Scorpion, which I had marked in the beginning of the night ride, had sunk out of sight in the West, but the Great and Little Bear swung high in twinkling beauty in the northern sky over the forest which I was approaching. The swamp never looked darker to me than it did that night ; and it seemed I never heard it sigh so much as, when stooping my head, I rode at eleven o'clock under its low-hanging branches into its black depths. The grating sound made by the mighty limbs overhead reminded me of a giant grinding his teeth. Away off to the left an owl hooted. It seemed the echoes would never die away. The cry was to the left, which, according to the Southern negro, means bad luck. There was another hoot from a different quarter, and the woods sighed as if in mortal pain. I followed the trail around a brake which could not be forded, the cypress knees looking in the dim starlight like headstones in a graveyard. I crossed a boggy slough, rode along its banks a mile, then on through cane-brakes and rustling palmettos, past the place where I had seen the startling vision.

I galloped on swiftly a mile or so, when suddenly from the left side of the road, where the trees were loftiest, and the shadows most dense, and there was a mass of tangled vines, a wild scream rang out on the air, followed immediately by a burst of maniacal laughter.

To say that my blood almost froze in my veins and a great horror filled me is to speak only the truth. But in five seconds it was all over as I recognized in the sounds, at first so startling, the peculiar laughter-like cries of our Southern owls. They first give a scream and then indulge in "haw-haws" horribly like the merriment of maniacs.

I observed that my horse never swerved at this sound. She recognized the natural quicker and better than I did.

Two miles farther put me in the neighborhood of "Dead Man's Bayou." As I drew near, looking carefully through the gloom for the road which led down to the ford, I suddenly saw through the trees ahead of me and to one side, the same colossal figure and white head I had encountered several hours before in the center of the forest. Stopping my horse I watched him with a beating heart, as he moved in a line almost parallel to the road and near the water's edge of the bayou. Like a flash I remembered my friend's warning, and said under my breath :

"Here is the crazy man."

Riding a little nearer, and again reining in my horse, I looked and listened. I saw at once he was trying to find a log or place where he could cross the stream, and I heard him moaning and muttering to himself. The bayou and the road approached each other at an angle, and I saw that the man would reach the ford ahead of me.

Here was a situation indeed. Still nearly a

mile from home, Dead Man's Bayou to cross, and a brawny negro lunatic in thirty feet of me!

Passing on ahead the man, still unconscious of my presence, went down to the bridge of rails or puncheons laid in the mud which made the ford; but as half of it was covered with rushing water fully four feet deep, his course was arrested, and again he gave that moaning sound. He moved up and down the bank, his gigantic figure looking even larger for the shadows, his white head floating spectrally in the gloom, and still muttering to himself.

What should I do?

Evidently the man was trying to cross the bayou. Unacquainted with the logs beneath, and ignorant of the depth of the water before him, he did not know what course to pursue.

I had a great battle within. Should I make a dash for the ford and leave this escaped lunatic in the woods? It certainly was the most prudent course. What would my slight form be in the grasp of this dangerous and powerful creature. Besides I was under no obligation, even if equally strong, to be hunting up and helping maniacs who were wandering about at midnight in a swamp.

But a feeling of pity began to rise in my heart.

The creature, whoever he might be, was in distress. I felt like running a risk to do a kindness. So, riding up suddenly out of the dark to him, I said:

"Can I help you across the water?"

The reply was so gibberish that a spasm of fear shot through me; but under the uncanny sound was the accent of suffering, and bending forward to scrutinize the features of the lunatic in the starlight, I thought I saw enough of need and bewilderment to be construed into a supplication for help. So speaking again to him cheerily and pointing to a fallen tree, I said:

"Stand on that log and get on behind me, and I will take you across."

The herculean Bedlamite mounted the log while I urged my animal closer, when, with hands outstretched, he stooped down and clutched me tightly about the throat. Merciful heavens! was he going to choke his benefactor.

No! evidently not this time. The hands pressed heavily down to steady his body, and he then stiffly swung himself astride the horse. The next moment he threw his arms around me and had me so pinioned that I could scarcely guide the animal! Another fear rose in my heart as I felt the grasp, while I mentally said:

" What a fool I am to be asking a giant lunatic to take a ride behind me in the woods at midnight."

The thought also flashed through me with a kind of grim humor :

" Who would have dreamed that having been warned about this very man, I would have him, a burly, crazy negro, hoisted up on my horse behind me, just two hours later. What would my friend think if he could see me now?"

But another moment reassured me as I noticed that the grasp was not of hate or fury, but, in a certain sense, one of helplessness.

Still, with sensations far from pleasant, I turned toward the ford. The horse fairly staggered under the heavy load as approaching the bridge I rode into the rushing torrent. She kept her footing with difficulty on the puncheons, which had grown smooth and slippery from the continual flow of water over them. The yellow current ran with a noise that rose above the floundering of the horse and the tossing of the tree branches overhead.

The faithful, but overloaded animal had reached the middle of the stream, when suddenly the left forefoot shot in between two of the sunken logs. The noble creature made a splendid effort to keep up and pull out, but in vain, and down all three of us went together into the flood. The horse struggled like a leviathan until the foot was extricated, and then plunged for the bank. The lunatic released his pinioning grasp of me and disappeared under the yellow waves. I made a precipitate dash for the sinking man, caught hold of his arms, which appeared thrust upward out of the water and, standing waist deep in the bayou, with great difficulty helped him to his feet.

In a few moments all three of us stood on the bank of the rushing stream, thoroughly saturated, and presenting a most remarkable appearance. The snorting, trembling horse, the white-headed, moaning lunatic, and myself, holding the animal with one hand and the crazy negro with the other, made a curious trio.

The rest of the journey to the house, which was almost a mile away, was made on foot, all three of us walking abreast along the star-lighted road, with white cotton fields on each side, and no sound breaking the stillness but the low, inarticulate noise made by the lunatic, and the footfalls of the faithful animal by my side.

In a little while the horse was comfortable in his stall in front of a full trough, the demented man was

left in kind hands in one of the negro cabins, where
food and dry clothing were given him, while I, in
the " Big House," tossed wakefully upon my bed
and reviewed the strange scenes of the last few
hours.

One thing was perfectly clear to me before falling asleep, and that was that in the face of the
perils which had been encountered, but one thing
had perished in the woods or drowned in the bayou,
and that was—my fear of the poor, crazy negro.

II.

SOME STRANGE THINGS.

NO truly enlightened individuals are what is called superstitious, anyhow it is warmly affirmed they are not. Sensible persons do not believe in ghosts. Nevertheless it is a curious fact that when people are gathered around the fire on a winter night and the wind is howling through the trees and moaning around the eaves of the house, and the fine snow is pecking like spirit fingers at the window pane as if for entrance, if some one, then and there, is asked to tell a ghost story, at once everybody becomes still, and one can hear a pin drop.

As the tale proceeds and the climax is being approached, you can hear indeed amused laughs and loud protests of unbelief, but the careful observer will note that the laughter sounds forced, the protest is too noisy, while a certain unmistakable interest in the narration, with flitting expressions on the face, show the vein of superstition is down there in spite of every disclaimer.

A picture in an illustrated paper of late edition reveals a group of little woolly-headed darkies, to whom the " Old Auntie " or " Granny " of the cabin has begun to tell a ghost story. The quick, stealthy glances over one another's shoulders at the black shadows in the yard, the growing white's of the rolling eyes, with the loud declaration, " Who's skeered o' ghosts," proclaimed the inward fear and secret belief in a manner to remind one of certain white people who with greater intelligence and therefore should know better, yet possess the same misgivings about visits from sheeted wanderers from the grave and the other world.

Still it is not to visible ghosts that we refer in this chapter, when we use the term and talk about "strange things."

We refer to occurrences and happenings of various sorts that are impressive, solemnizing, mysterious, hard to account for, and some that are never explained in our present lives.

One of these smaller mysteries took place when the writer was a boy. It was the custom of his mother to take a walk each afternoon about sunset with the children. One evening on our return we were told by the servant that a gentleman had called in our absence, walked into the parlor, took a seat in one of the large high-back cushioned arm chairs, tilted it back, fell over backward with it, turned a complete somersault on the floor, rose up, went to

the hat rack, took his hat and departed without a
word, and without leaving a card or his name.

All our questionings could get no more than the
facts just narrated from the deeply impressed servant girl, who saw nothing amusing in the occurrence, though some of the family laughed quite
heartily.

To this day the incident remains a profound
mystery in the family history. If it happened to
one of our gentleman friends, he never allowed the
fact to be known, so that the strange occurrence
was handed down through the years as that of an
unknown man falling backward out of the big arm
chair, rolling on the floor and then departing without a word. "The man who rolled on the floor
out of the chair" became like a member of the
family in some respects; but it was also noticeable
that we children did not care to be alone in the parlor after dark, for a long while afterwards. Who
could tell but that same chair would go over backward again when the room was dark and no one but
a little boy was around. And what if he should see
a human body tumbling toward him on the floor, and
flinging back somersaults as it came. No indeed,
this was not to be thought of for a moment, and so the
children agreed unanimously that it was best to stay

away from that part of the family mansion after nightfall ; and though they insisted they were not afraid, yet with all that, it seemed wiser, more prudent and certainly safer to stay away.

*   *   *   *   *   *   *   *

Another strange occurrence took place several years ago in one of our Southern States. The circumstance can be vouched for by a dozen reliable people. A certain very prominent clergyman died at the age of eighty. He passed away in a town in one State and was to be buried four hundred miles away in the capital of another State. His family of sons and daughters, now in middle life, prepared to attend the funeral. One of the sons, whom we will call George, lived in a town midway between the two places. As he had recently come from a western city the family had not seen him in twenty years. He was duly telegraphed as to the time the train would pass the town of B———, where he lived, with the body of his father and with several of his brothers and sisters on the way to the city of C———, one hundred miles farther south, where the interment was to take place.

As the train stopped at B———, George came on board just as they expected. He kissed them all, and sat down first by one and then another of his brothers and sisters, asking a number of questions about his father. As they had not seen him for years they were surprised to find him so little changed.

Just as the train started to go, he arose and said good-bye. The entire family party were astonished and told him they thought he was going with them to C——— to the funeral.

He replied that he would meet them at C———, and they saw him, after saying this, get off the cars at B———. Several hours afterward, as the train dashed into C———, they happened to look out of the window as they rolled into the depot and saw George leaning against the building as if waiting for them. When, filled with wonder, they went up to him they discovered to their amazement that he looked twenty years older than he did when they saw him a few hours before in B———.

He welcomed them kindly ; and when with rapid utterance and wondering eyes they asked him how he could be in C——— when they had left him in B———, he quietly replied that he had not been in B——— !

All kinds of investigation have been unable to clear up this mystery. Those who have heard the strange circumstance have put the very questions the reader will.

First, was not the man who came on the train at B—— George's son, who looked like his father? No, for George had no son, and more than that his brothers and sisters knew him, and he spoke of his dead father.

Second, may not George have jumped on the train after getting off and gone on with them to C——? No, they noticed him when the train pulled out and saw him walk away. Moreover if he had come on the train, how could he have been at C—— leaning against the depot building waiting for them.

Third, may he not have taken another train and beaten them to C—— ?

No, for they were on the fast train and there was none other for eight hours. Besides if this had been so, what was it that put twenty years upon him in three hours' time! It has been one of those happenings of a weird, mysterious nature that has not yet, and may never be cleared up in this world. People most interested in the matter have been unable to do anything with it as to its solution or explanation. It is one of the strange things of life.

*　　*　　*　　*

Another most mysterious occurrence took place during one of the writer's visits to a southern town. It transpired in a dwelling which sat back from the street, in the middle of the block, having a number of large magnolia trees almost hiding the front view. It was a large building, two stories in height, with a heavily pillared front gallery running the entire length of the house. The shadows about the building were dense even in day time, by reason of the magnolias in front, and the forest trees filling the side and back yards. Some shrubbery struggled for life in the side yard, between the weeds beneath, and the sun-hiding branches of the trees above.

For many years the house had been occupied by a middle aged married couple. After the husband died the widow, to dissipate in some measure the loneliness of the old shadowy homestead, allowed a young couple with their infant child and a sixteen year old nurse to board with her.

For awhile the silence and gloom of the dwelling, its large empty rooms, its long, winding front gallery disappearing around a distant corner of the building, greatly depressed the new comers; but after a few weeks they became in a measure accustomed to it all.

One night the three adults of the house went out to a public speaking in the central part of the town, leaving the baby asleep upon the bed, and the colored nurse girl in the same room to care for her.

The other servants had gone to their own homes in a distant part of the town, and the big house was locked up.

In leaving, the young mother promised the nurse not to be gone long, and so intended, but the exercises were lengthier than she had anticipated, and so when they returned, clicked the front gate behind them and walked up the graveled path overshadowed by the dark magnolias, the town clock was solemnly tolling the hour of twelve.

On bidding the elderly lady good night in the hall, the young mother turned to her bed-room, and glancing at once toward her bed where she had laid the baby failed to see the child, but instead noticed that the covering had been drawn down and then thrown back towards the pillows, so that the child might possibly be under it.

The lamp had been turned low and was burning dimly, so that the room was full of shadows. The nurse was sound asleep on the floor on a pallet. Walking quickly to the lamp the mother turned up the light, passed to the bed and pulling back the cover was horrified to find her child bespattered with blood, and on taking her up in her arms discovered she was unconscious.

With a wild scream that rang through the house

she brought the child closer to the light, and saw on the right cheek the marks of a double row of teeth that had bitten deeply into the flesh, had almost met, and been withdrawn, leaving the cheek with the appearance of an apple that had been bitten into, and yet the piece not removed.

At this new discovery the mother's shrieks became so piercing and frequent that the nurse awoke, and soon after the lady of the house came rushing in. The nurse was unmistakably shocked and grieved, and was sent flying to give the alarm to the nearest neighbors. Meantime the husband had come in, and he with the two women labored with the child to restore consciousness, and in so doing made two other startling discoveries; one was that the child's clothing was badly torn as if she had been dragged through the shrubbery, and on the left temple was a contusion as if a blow had been dealt the little innocent.

By this time a number of neighbors in various stages of dress and undress had arrived, and partook of the horror and pain which filled the hearts of the family. The nurse could give no explanation of the strange and awful occurrence. Her sleepy eyes, unquestionable amazement, and evident sorrow and the condition of the body removed every suspicion from the mind that she had anything to do with the ghastly deed. Moreover a glance at her mouth and teeth showed that the bite could not have been given by her. The imprint or rather deep incision of teeth on the child's cheek showed that a much larger mouth had done the work.

In due time physicians arrived, but could throw but little more light on the matter than was already possessed. The baby had been struck on the temple, bitten on the cheek and dragged or carried through the briars somewhere. In addition to these facts evident to all, the men of medicine were able to state that the biter was not an animal but a human being, and not a small, but a large person. After this, all else was a deep, dark mystery. Questions arose to every lip which could not be answered. Some were these.

" What could possibly have been the motive leading to the crime?"

" What could have torn the clothing of the baby? "

" If, as it seemed, the garments were torn by briars, why was the child carried through the shrubbery ?"

" Why was it borne from the house at all?" That it was carried off was evident from the clothing.

"Then, if taken away from the house, why was it brought back?"

"Still again, why was the child so entirely covered up with the bed clothes? Was it to smother its cries, or was the intention to kill by suffocation?"

These and other questions were asked by the horror-stricken group of friends and neighbors of one another, and there was no one who could answer them. There was abundant speculation indeed, but conjecture is not facts, and it was facts that were wanted. At this juncture the doctors made two other discoveries that only heightened the mystery One was that the blow on the temple was evidently not made to kill, but to stun. The other was that after the infliction of the bite, there was unmistakable evidence of suction by lips.

The last feature of the case brought forth from the large assembled company not only expressions of horror and disgust, but explanations about Voodooism, etc.

But there were the stubborn facts before them of a house with barred windows, and thick heavy doors safely locked up, with not a soul in the building but the baby and girl nurse, and not a sign of a broken window or forced door.

The clothing of the nurse was carefully examined for thorn rents, but there was not a vestige upon which to hang suspicion. Whoever carried the child through the briars one thing was certain, that it was not the nurse.

Of course there was a prompt and thorough search of the grounds. Aroused and indignant men went into every dark corner of the magnolia grove, penetrated the shadowy side and back yards, beat the shrubbery, examined every out-house and visited the cabins in the neighborhood, of suspicious character, especially among the negroes.

But it was all in vain. The night-horror remained a mystery then, and continues such after an interval of over twenty years.

The occurrence cast a profound gloom over the community for quite a while. Mothers clasped their little ones to their breast with a blended feeling of protecting love and fear. Few of them for a long time after that would leave their homes after nightfall. Imagination pictured a human monster creeping over walls and crouching in gardens at night, with the mad desire of kidnaping babies, biting them, and sucking their veins dry of blood.

Officers of the law and private detectives worked on the case with the greatest zeal and ingenuity. Old negro men and women were viewed with the same readiness to fasten guilt upon them, as in the days of the Salem witchcraft craze. But no one was able to find a single clew to lead to the discovery of the human dragon or vampire. So after many months of surmisings of all kinds, and efforts of every description, all hope of detection died, and the night occurrence in the old house in the magnolia grove became by common consent and judgment, one of the dark mysteries of time, and only to be unvailed and made known at the Last Day.

The matter, however, led to the removal of the family from the house, and for all we know it is still empty. A gloomy building before as barely seen through the great, solemn, rustling trees, it became gloomier. To many it seemed positively uncanny.

No one liked to pass along its long paling fence after night. A feeling that something grisly and ghastly was hiding among the trees, or looking out from the darkened windows of the room where the baby had been attacked, made numbers cross the street and walk on the other side.

The old magnolia trees grew thicker and taller

after this, and shot their branches over the path in such a downward and interlacing way, that any one looking from the front gate toward the house could only see the lower steps leading up to the gallery. However there seemed to be few indeed who cared to look : and so the old mansion was left to the gloom and silence, and to the possession of the fearful secret of that memorable autumn night.

III.

WHY THEY WEPT.

Prominent ministers in a church have aspired to still higher positions. They wished to add to their fame other things. Besides had they not read "If a man desire the office of a bishop he desireth a good work;" a free translation of the last three words reading "a good thing."

One aspirant may be a natural born politician laying his plans wisely and well, without offensive public exposure of the design in the mind and desire of the heart. Ardent friends and admirers with calculating eye upon hunter, dogs, and fox, become in a sense whippers in, and look forward not without anticipation and strong confidence as well, to the capture of the "brush," at a certain quadrennial season when hunters will be out in force and a grand drive take place.

Another aspirant convinces his church that he has remarkable executive and administrative ability. Still another places the whole denomination under obligation by untangling some knotty church question, and throwing great light on that darkly profound thing, ecclesiastical jurisprudence, while a fourth lays the church under an additional burden of gratitude, by the removal of a load quite different from the other, but not the less heavy, mortifying and even crushing.

It matters not what the service may have been, whether it required the working of the hands or the heels, the brains or the tongue ; yet some things are not done in a corner, nor can they be kept in a corner. It moves the Sanhedrim ; it touches the Council of the Seventy in a tender place ; while the Elders and Scribes are sure to write and talk about the affair.

Who but a prophet could forsee that the same aforesaid distinguished and grateful men when they came together in one of their great gatherings would offer some " whereases " and " be it resolveds," twist their appreciation into a garland of certain gratifying shape and place it on the brow of one who had sky-rocketed his name and ricoched his body over the country for a space of time covering the waxing and waning of many moons, not to speak of the suns.

There are however still others who do not lift a hand, so to speak, to obtain one of these high offices. They would feel degraded if they did anything on the outside looking to their elevation to this dignity. They simply long for it in the mind. It is an inner instead of an outer race for the goal.

Now when through plans or no plans at all, certain aspirants get the garlands mentioned, when after a little snow storm of ballots they are declared elected, even if they never get saved, it has been observed that without exception they burst into tears!

The whole thing is so sudden! so unexpected! so bewildering! Then doubtless some of them feel so unworthy, and the responsibility is so great! Then leadership is such a life of loneliness! so overworked! so misunderstood! so unappreciated?

In view of all this who can wonder at the weeping.

It is felt by a number of the brethren that the tears of successful candidates do them great credit. Others remark that there are certain conditions when it is a positive luxury and delight to weep. Still others have been known to say with meaning looks and smiles that they would be willing to exchange places with the elected martyrs in order to shed such tears. And still others with peculiar construction of the intellect and sensibilities utterly fail to see what there is to cry over at such a time.

Among the observers of several such scenes was a man who described them to the writer. The conversation led almost insensibly up to a little humble talk about Psychology, the philosophy of tears, the thin wall between laughter and crying, etc., etc.

At last the writer, after a thoughtful pause in which he took down a picture from the wall of memory, brushed the dust from it, and held it so as to obtain a better light upon the scene, spoke suddenly,

" I have the explanation."

Then, after another moment's deliberation, with an unmistakable humorous twinkling in the eyes, he said :

" My childhood was spent in Yazoo City, Mississippi. My mother had a lady friend, a Mrs. R——, who lived several miles in the country and often visited us.

One day on returning from school, after loitering somewhat on the street on my homeward way, I was informed by my mother that if I had come home from school promptly I would have been in time to have accepted an invitation to go on a steamboat trip to Vicksburg. That Mrs. R—had come by in her carriage with her two boys on her way to the river landing where she would take the steamboat at 6 o'clock. That Mrs. R——wanted me to go with her sons and had waited a full half hour for me, but as the steamer left at 6 p. m. she could wait no longer, and had to leave without me.

In exact correspondence of facts and accurate detail, the same bitter history was related by my brothers and sisters and the servants. In like manner spake they all. As the funeral discourse and services proceeded, divided up among a number, the heart of the ten year old lad went steadily down toward his shoes, while a great aching, swelling lump ascended the other way and lodged in his throat. The world looked black indeed at that moment to the little school boy, and he was convinced that the future held nothing for him but despair.

If there was anything he passionately loved and admired it was a steamboat. If there was any place he craved to see it was Vicksburg. He had been to several picnics on the shores of a woodland lake, and to a Fourth of July celebration on the riverside, and been on an hour's excursion on a stern-wheeler, but here was a three days' trip on a beautiful side wheel steamer. He had lived in a town of two thousand inhabitants, but Vicksburg had twelve thousand, and sat by the bank of a river one mile wide, and had from fifty to one hundred steamboats loading and unloading, coming and going at her wharfs all the time. Had he not heard of all these things and much more of its many wonders? And now that the chance of seeing with the eye and hearing with the ear, these sights and sounds, had been given only to be lost, dashed to the ground, taken away forever,—alas! it was too hard! What need to live! What was left in life anyhow!

The mother stood looking at the silent but grief-stricken lad, and the unhappy boy gazed in a hopeless sort of way at the wall before him, which seemed to shut in and end every prospect in the world.

At last trying with a dry tongue to moisten equally dry lips, the lad asked in a feeble, die-away voice.

"Did the mother think it was too late to try to overtake Mrs. R——and her boys?"

"Yes," came the reply, "they are now at the boat by this time."

"Would it be too late to reach the boat still?"

The answer was that it was now after five o'clock, the boat left at six, the "landing" was a mile away, and he had to be dressed.

The head sank lower, and the lump **got** larger.

"Would she be willing to let him try to reach the boat?"

"Yes, but she knew it was no earthly use to try. She also said that all this came from loitering and not coming directly home from school. That it was evidently a judgment on him for his carelessness ; and anyhow it was a lesson which she fervently trusted he would never forget the longest day he lived."

He felt and admitted that he would never forget it. Moreover, if he could get forgiveness on the part of home and heaven for his misdeed, he never would do so any more, etc., etc.

The boy's grief and disappointment seemed suddenly to put double sets of hands on the bodies of the family, and in less time than it takes to tell it, his face had been scoured and rubbed, his hair brushed and curled, and a neat fitting black suit, of jacket, knee pantaloons and broad white collar was upon him. And now with his cap jammed by loving hands almost over his ears to make it stick, a small carpet bag containing some underwear thrust into his hand, and a dozen kisses aimed at him and most of them missing him, he was told to run, if not for his life, then at least for the boat!

They were synonymous with the boy. And he did run. He tarried for no second bidding. The little legs fairly twinkled over the ground. Two blocks away as he whirled around a corner, a glance over his shoulder revealed the entire family standing before the front gate, and gazing after him.

He did not need this sight however to nerve him to greater exertion. The steamboat and Vicksburg were amply sufficient.

So he ran ; ran until the breath came in great gasps, till the blood sung in his ears, and till the heart which had arisen from the feet now appeared to have concluded to beat its way out of the body through the ribs.

Owing to the weight of the traveling bag, and the long run, the lad had now and then to slacken his speed to get his breath, but the fear of being left would act like a fresh stimulant upon him, and he, with laboring respiration, and heart torn with conflicting emotions, would rush ahead again.

Finally he reached the center of the town, which was half way from his mother's house to the wharf, when he heard the solemn toll of the steamboat bell signifying to the public that ten minutes remained before her departure. The boy partly through shame of being seen running on the street, and partly through exhaustion had subsided into a rapid walk, but the solemn notes of the bell sounded so much like the funeral knell of the Vicksburg trip that he broke forth into new efforts though his limbs were all trembling and his brain fairly spun around.

There was much smiling on the streets as the lad with crimson face, loud breathing, and carpet bag thumping against his legs, sped as well as staggered on his way to the river. It was evident to all that the lad was trying to get somewhere whether he ever succeeded or not.

Various calls and cries were uttered, and considerable advice given gratis to him by men lounging on street corners, or sprawling in chairs and settees in front of stores, hotels and the livery stable.

" Better give it up my lad !"

" No use sonny !"

" Too late my boy !"

" She'll be gone before you can reach the wharf, youngster !"

" She's tolling her last bell now !"

" Better wait for the next trip !"

Etc., etc., etc.

The lad made no reply to any of these remarks, partly for lack of breath, and partly because the end in view allowed no time for rejoinder, repartee or any other kind of conversation. Action was what was wanted, and according to Demosthenese, action many times repeated.

Farther down the street he heard the bell tolling again ; this time three strokes signified that five minutes were left. Oh if the captain and passengers knew how hard he was trying to reach the boat, they surely would wait five minutes more and save a boy from a broken heart.

As the panting and now fairly exhausted lad turned out of Main Street upon the broad wharf front, with its long, brick warehouses, piles of cotton and rows of boxes and barrels, he could see the boat two hundred yards away, still at the shore, with great volumes of black smoke pouring out of the top of the big smoke stacks. The pilot was at the wheel, the captain was on the top deck, a crowd of passengers stood in the forecastle observing every detail of the last scene. The mate was thundering orders to the deck hands, who with a sing-song " Yo-ho, Yo-e-oh, " were drawing in the big stage plank. The side wheels of the steamer were giving a restless occasional turn, churning the water

into a foam and sending it in waves to the shore.
A single narrow plank connected the boat with the
bank, and a negro stood ready on the shore to cast
off the last rope which bound the vessel to the
wharf.

All this was taken in like a flash, by the hot,
gasping, crimson-faced, hoping, fearing, but still
striving lad, as holding to the carpet sack, he actually staggered his way through piles of cotton
bales and merchandise, across the rock-covered
landing.

The big bell tolled a single time, the negro cast
off the rope, the wheels plowed into the water with
the roar of escaping steam, the boat began to move
backward while the deck hands seized the solitary
plank to draw it on board, when the lad, up to this
time unnoticed by the crew or passengers, put his
foot upon it, made one desperate surge, and in the
midst of astonished looks and exclamations, ran or
rather tottered along the unsteady length and literally tumbled on the deck of the boat when it was
fully six feet from shore.   At once rising up from
the edge of the vessel he staggered to the foot of
the main stairway, sank down on the first step, with
his carpet sack between his knees, and BURST INTO
TEARS !

Does any one ask why he wept? The reply is that there were a number of motives at work in his heart of an agitating character ; but the main cause of the overflow was that HE HAD GOTTEN THERE !

And so he mopped his face, and wept freely ; and bowed his head, and wept some more He could not reply to questions propounded to him by those standing around. He was too busy weeping.

And yet the psychologist, or close student of human nature could have said, that is not the sound of mourning, but the voice of singing do I hear.

No, the boy was not sad. He was no sadder than Jacob was when he kissed Rachel and lifted up his voice and wept. The lad was in tears, but they were happy tears, relieving tears, delicious tears. He had made the trip, carpet sack and all. He had gotten there. He was, so to speak, elected.

*　　*　　*　　*

There was silence between the two friends for a few moments and then the writer said :

"Do you think you have light on the tears shed those mornings after the election?"

" I certainly do. I can see the long run, the thumping carpet bag and what it stands for, the fear of being left, the warning bell, the narrow plank, and at last the getting on board, the sitting down on the first convenient bench or chair, and the relieving burst of tears in the thought, I have made the run, I am on the boat; henceforth there is laid up for me a splendid position and fine salary all the days of my life.''

Another pause; when my friend said:

'' I do not question but there are many tears for which men get credit, that could never stand the analysis of heaven.''

''Undoubtedly. This is the case with a first successful effort on platform or in pulpit. With some temperaments, the instant the labor is over, there is a decided inclination to have a cry. Then there is a certain feeling of astonishment, and self gratulation with others that they got through at all; and these mental states lead right up to a weeping fit with many people. But in these and other cases, the principle is the same. Some boat has been reached after a hard struggle; and the relief is so great with the conscious sudden ending of a prolonged strain, and the blissful certainty that they are on board, and need to run no more—all this, by the working of a natural law produces a gush of sweet, delicious, relieving tears.''

'' Precisely so,'' said my friend, and then look-

ing up with a smile of amusement he said, " I suppose the longer the run, the heavier and bigger the
carpet-sack, and the finer the boat—the deeper,
sweeter and more enjoyable will be the weeping."

" Undoubtedly," I replied.

" Then may heaven help us all," said he.

"Amen and Amen," said I.

IV.

BY THE word retribution we mean a kind of moral boomerang, and in this case a ghastly occurrence strikingly and shockingly similar to some fearful act committed upon another in the past months or years. Whoever has given the matter even slight attention can not but be impressed with the fact of such happenings, running like a black thread in the pattern of human life. After awhile we discover that not only curses, but deeds themselves come home like chickens to roost. In figurative language a bullet is shot which kills a man, and then, under this strange law of retribution, plows its way on through the murdered body, speeds on its mysterious way, striking here and glancing there, yet always in search for the person who fired the ball, until at last it encircles the earth in its flight, gets back to the place where it started, finds the slayer, pierces and kills him, and then falls in the dust to lie still forever!

The fact of retribution crops out in the Bible in numerous places. Jacob deceived his father with a garment sprinkled with blood, and long afterward was deceived by his sons in an identical manner. The brethren of Joseph laid violent hands upon him, and lo ! years subsequently violent hands were laid upon themselves, and the very similarity of grasp instantly brought back by association the memory of the past, and they in sudden agony of mind remembered Joseph, and said one to another, " we are verily guilty concerning our brother, in that we saw the anguish of his soul, when he besought us, and we would not hear ; therefore is this distress come upon us."

The man who invented that instrument of torment, the body-rack, died upon it ; and he who gave the guillotine to the world perished by its deadly blade.

We knew a person who took advantage of another, shooting him when he was not expecting an assault, and emptying his gun in his back. The unfortunate being fell in front of a certain office on the leading street, and was placed upon a lounge taken out of the building, and was carried home to die.

In less than three years this murderer was himself killed by another man, and the remarkable features of the case were that he was not looking for an attack, was shot in the back, was attacked on the very spot where he had slain his victim, fell down before the same office, and was carried home on the same lounge to die.

A still more striking instance occurred in the county were the writer was born and raised.

For several years the author of this book was connected with a country store some ten or twelve miles from the nearest town. Queer and wild characters, both white and black, used to visit the place on trading and loafing expeditions. An exceedingly interesting book could be written on the strange events that took place there in the course of the three or four years of our stay. What with occasional horse-racing, drinking, fighting and some shooting, there were days that were anything but desirable and enjoyable.

Among the rough looking men who visited the store was a tall, lank, sandy-haired man, with prominent cheek bones and sunken jaws and eyes. He always carried a gun with him, and which he never laid aside. Standing up, it stood by his side; sitting down, it was placed across his lap as though ready to be used. He had a weary, uneasy look, and scarcely ever smiled. Repeatedly the writer has seen him leaning for hours against the front wall of the store, with his hands encircling the up-right barrel of his gun, and without speaking a a word, taking in what was going on around him, with no lighting up of the face or responsiveness whatever. After awhile he would purchase a plug or sack of tobacco, or some ammunition and ride off as silently and as spectrally as he came. The man had a history well known to many. He was a mur-derer. There had been something in the deed and there was something in the man that made people perfectly willing to give him a wide berth.

He had fifteen years before been employed as an overseer on a large cotton plantation. He lived in a two-roomed cabin near the forest which skirted the field. The owner, a southern gentleman named North, would occasionally leave his hill place and visit his swamp plantation for a few days, and when he did so would stay in the cabin of his overseer, whose name was Oldham. Mr. North was greatly given to practical jokes and especially a spirit of teasing; and when he had taken a mint julip or whisky toddy he was apt to carry his humor at the expense of another to excess. In one of his visits to the cabin he made his manager, Oldham, the target of his verbal arrows,

The man was possessed of a morbidly sensitive

nature, and knowing nothing of a polished social
life, was unable to defend himself with word weap-
ons similar to those that North was using upon him.
He was conscious of but one power superior to the
man who was laughing at him, and that was brute
force. Construing the badinage, which he did not
altogether understand, into insult, and realizing his
helplessness in language, and as fully conscious of
his might in bone and muscle, the tiger nature suddenly flashed into his eyes and sprang forth in his
hands, and in another minute a dreadful deed was
committed that morning upon the puncheon floor of
the cabin gallery.

There was but one witness of the ghastly act, and
it was done so quickly that he had not time to prevent. The infuriated overseer caught his teasing
employer up in his hands and dashed him upon the
floor, then seizing his heavy rifle he brought the
heavy barrel, weighing fully twenty-five pounds,
down with a terrible crash upon the skull. The
smitten man trying to arise from the floor gave
one glance of horror at his slayer as the gun descended, and sank at his feet under the blow, without a word, and died almost instantly.

Oldham had killed a true friend.

The unhappy man fled from the country, and

was gone for years. But by enlisting in the army during the Civil War he was pardoned, and after the surrender at Appomattox returned to his old neighborhood in the hills.

He came back a man of few words and with a set air of melancholy in face and manner. He rarely spoke. He seemed to be like one expecting calamity or judgment to overtake him, and was constantly on the alert for self-protection and deliverance.

Years went by; over twenty since he killed North. He was now approaching fifty, but looked as if he was sixty. It was during these days we would see him in his occasional visits to the store.

One day the tiger in him was aroused by some real or fancied injury done him by a negro man who lived a couple of miles from his home. So saddling his mule and placing his rifle on the pummel of the saddle he rode toward the cabin of the colored man to take vengeance.

The negro saw him coming, and the two men met on the road near the yard gate. Both were armed. Oldham lifted his gun to shoot, when his animal taking fright at the sudden motion swerved to one side and threw his rider to the ground. In falling Oldham's foot became entangled in the stirrup and he could not at once arise. The negro saw his advantage, and running quickly picked up Oldham's fallen gun, and standing over his prostrate foe, raised the heavy barrel high in the air before the gaze of the panic-stricken man.

It was only for an instant! But who can tell what was in that moment to the man on the gronnd. Here was retribution indeed! Here was what he had been watching against, and flying from for over twenty years. He was being slain exactly as he had killed North. The negro was standing over him as he had stood over his victim. He was about to be struck with the heavy barrel of the rifle as he had struck his old time friend. He himself was looking up with horror, even as North had looked up at him in horror. He had just one moment to live, as his employer had, and——crash!

The heavy gun barrel had broken in the skull of the unfortunate man; the unprepared soul was swept into eternity; and the murderer and the murdered were together once more, after the flight of nearly a quarter of a century.

V.

WE LEFT the train two hours after midnight in a town in the mountains of North Carolina. It was bitterly cold, and as we registered at the desk of the hotel office we requested the clerk to have us a good fire made at once in the room to which we had been assigned.

There was a prompt answer that it should be done, a pompous clang of the bell which died away in the dark, chilly passages of the hostelry, and finally the tardy appearance of a sleepy-looking colored boy of about twenty.

The order was given to have a fire in "59" at once : and the writer of these lines tarried for at least fifteen minutes in the dingy office, adorned with State and Railroad maps, in order that the chill might be taken off "59" and so one's health and life might be assured.

When I finally entered the apartment given to me, I discovered that "the fire" so grandly ordered consisted of several delicate sticks of kindling, a piece of brown paper on the sticks and a wash pan full of coal dust on the paper. A few tongues of flame were creeping over the edge of the paper apparently peeping at, and examining the black looking powder, as if in doubt whether it would burn or explode.

Turning to the negro boy who had created this fiction or mild representation of a fire, I found he was silently but fixedly gazing like myself at the artifice.

At last I spoke.

"Do you call that a fire?"

The simple faced soul rubbed his head meditatively, showed most of his teeth and replied.

"Well, Boss, I tell yer jes' how tis, we sont for a ka'yr load o' coal, and when dat ka'yr come, t'want nuthin but dus'."

Here was light thrown on the situation, if not heat. The blame rested not on the fire maker, nor the clerk, or the hotel, but on some distant coal company who had "sont dus'" instead of coal and were now all unconscious of the suffering they were inflicting on innocent travelers.

After a few moments more of conjoint, silent inspection of the modest glimmer in the grate, the tall lank youth, who had been lingering with the door knob in his hand, and considerable sympathy

in his face, began to withdraw. Closing the door
on his neck, so as to put his body in the hall out of
sight, while his head hung spectrally midway
between the floor and ceiling, he said,

"I don't speck dey gwine ter charge you fur
dat fire."

Having uttered this oracular message, the round,
black, woolly head disappeared, the door closed,
and I was left alone, hovering over the fire place
and shaking for two distinct reasons.

Stooping at last to move one of the splinters and
thereby assist the struggling flames, suddenly there
was a landslide of the black coal dust, and the fire
was out! Pompeii was never more certainly covered up and hidden from mortal sight than was
the paper and kindling construction buried in the
cavernous grate. Moreover, it vanished from view
much more rapidly than did the doomed city of
the plain.

There was nothing to do but to undress quickly,
vault between the icy sheets, and seek in sleep for
forgetfulness of present discomforts and woes, and
this was done.

But one thought of mild comfort rested in the
mind above the chattering teeth, before unconsciousness came. The thought was born of the

farewell remark of the negro as he swung and nodded his head in the air.

"I don't speck dey gwine ter charge you fur dat fire."

Smiling and drowsily repeating, "I don't speck so either," the writer, in spite of a frozen mattress, frosty sheets, and an icy counterpane, fell asleep from weariness, if not from comfort, and knew no more until morning.

*　　*　　*　　*　　*

In a small town in Mississippi I spent several days in what proved a mere apology of a hotel. The tavern, as some called it, opened upon a great square, which was treelesss and houseless ; and also opened itself much of the time to raw winter winds, which freely visited the halls and rooms through the accommodating doors.

There was nothing to see without doors, as a compensation for the lack of comfort within the hostelry. I would have fared badly but for a character I encountered during my brief stay.

He was a colored youth, and one of the waiters in the dining-room. He became quite communicative in his visits to the rooms of myself and a gentleman friend accompaning me. He not only left coal, kindling and fresh water for us, but various interesting facts concerning himself. In fact he seemed more concerned about the latter than the former. To be really truthful, he was burdened until he delivered himself of various biographical features which pressed upon his mind. His perfect self-complacency, not to say tremendous satisfaction with, and approval of, himself, as exhibited in manner, facial expression and words, was something beyond description.

He had been a student in a "Colored College" in the State. He had acquired a smattering of knowledge, which he strove to reproduce with the disadvantage of a tongue not over skillful in the matters of expression and pronunciation. So he uttered some memorable things. One of his statements was that, in vacation times, "He left the Universe and lectured."

He, of course, meant the university by the word universe, but we thought, with a smile, of the many lecturers and speakers who, in the indulgence of the speculative and imaginative, do truly and really leave the universe.

Being asked by my friend what his subjects were in his lecture tours, he replied that one was, "The Effects of Morals as They Stand Alone." We suggested as a paraphrase the sentence, "The loneliness of morals," and thought that certain parts of the country had been struck again.

He was asked one morning as he leaned, or rather hung on the end of the mantlepiece, " If he ever reached a place where thought and words failed him in his public addresses." His delightful reply was :

"Ever since I have been twelve years old, I have had the gift of sitting down when I run out of something to say."

Truly, I thought, here is one of the lost arts, and of all secrets which have perished, this could least have been spared. I could but think of the unspeakable relief that would be afforded, and the joy which would fill men's hearts, if all speakers had the gift of sitting down when they run out of ideas and facts.

On another occasion our waiter, who was becoming interested in the revival services, said that " he had heard some ministers preach on the two works of grace, regeneration and sanctification, but for his life he couldn't see where they made any extinguished difference."

This last statement opened up a great field to the vision which was filled with human figures who wore beaver hats, and were dressed in long-skirted black coats, bearing a solitary row of numerous buttons.

We saw the Zinzendorfian brother, who insists he was sanctified when he was converted, and persists in calling himself a Methodist. We beheld the man who had crowded definitions and meanings into the word regeneration which it never possessed. We noticed the preacher who lifted regeneration so high that it was lost in sanctification. The next glance fell on another who pulled sanctification down to such an extent that it was merged into and swallowed up in regeneration. We saw the time-serving brother who did not want to give offence, and so toned down, trimmed up, changed Scriptural words and phrases and used instead terms of human manufacture. And behold in every case, in their presentation of the two beautiful and blessed doctrines of the Bible, there was no ''extinguished difference.'' They themselves had extinguished the difference.

VI.

THE FACE AT THE WINDOW.

THE author was once visiting in a poverty-stricken part of a city where, under Conference appointment, he was stationed. While sitting on the steps of an humble home exchanging some words with the good woman who lived there, she happened to speak of a time in the " fifties " when the town was scourged by yellow fever, and hundreds of citizens died. She gave an incident of the plague which made a profound impression on the writer, and is here transcribed as a pen picture.

She said that with the daily increasing death-rate, a darker gloom fell upon the devoted place. The only sounds to be heard were the tolling of bells, which by and by were discontinued on account of the depressing effect upon the sick, and the roll of the wheels of hearse or wagon going with the dead to the cemetery or returning therefrom. Most of the people who had not fled from town, remained shut up in their houses, and only now and then a passer could be seen.

One day she was standing at her window when suddenly she saw a wagon driven rapidly up in front of a large empty house just opposite her own. Two men leaped out and lifting a third man, a yellow fever patient, from the wagon, they bore him into the house.

They next carried in a cot, and then she saw them place the sick man upon it, close the door, and leave the house. Either the men forgot the poor creature, or they themselves were stricken down with the plague, but for some reason they never came back, and the man was left alone and uncared for. The woman could see that he was in a bare unfurnished room of the vacant house, and as hour followed hour and no one came to his relief, her distress was great, and she could not keep from the window, through which she looked across the street toward the forgotten sufferer. She could just see the lower end of the cot, and so only a part of the human form which rested upon it.

Humanity as well as Christianity pleaded with her to go over and help the forsaken man, but she was afraid and could not. Still she could not banish the thought of the loneliness and need of the sufferer, and so she found herself repeatedly at the window looking with a heavy heart and condemning conscience in the direction of the unfortunate being.

In the afternoon of the second day, while at her old post, looking for the hundredth time in that direction, suddenly she saw the sick man arise, stagger to the window, and leaning against it, look up and down the street. *He then turned a steadfast gaze toward her, and their eyes met !*

A great horror filled her as she felt the appealing eyes of the dying man fixed on her. She said she came near dropping on the floor in a swoon.

In another moment the unhappy being turned and walked back toward his bed, fell upon it, and lay motionless. She remained rooted, spellbound, horror-stricken to the spot for quite a while, a prey to the most conflicting and agonizing feelings.

Two hours afterward several men drove up to the house, went in, and found the man was dead !

*　　*　　*　　*　　*　　*

We will never forget the distress of the woman as she related the above history. It had been nearly a quarter of a century ago, but the scene seemed still fresh before her, and the horror as great as if it had only recently happened.

We have since then thought how the melancholy occurrence illustrates facts and conditions which should come, and does come very near to us all.

We thought of those men and women who have life burdens and heart sickness to carry, that most people do not seem to have noticed. The wagon with the men in it drive off and do not come back, carriages roll by, pedestrians do not so much as glance in the direction of the sufferer, those living nearest by fail to recognize that a tragedy is going on, that a life with all its hope, strength and possibilities is passing away, and dying unattended and unrelieved.

Who has not had such a look turned upon him from some passing face on the street, or from an acquaintance in the social circle. Who has not seen the man at the window; and recognized an awful sorrow in the countenance, and felt the silent appeal of the eyes.

And yet we have allowed these wretched ones to go back to their lonely lots and lie down in unrelieved suffering to die.

Chatterton, the poetic marvel of England, died of starvation. A gifted authoress in this country of plenty, died several years ago of actual want. Her diary is heartbreaking to read, as she describes her hunger pangs. A number of suicides have left letters with the statement that they were alone in the world, no one seemed to care for them, they could not get work, and so there was nothing left except to die.

A friend of the writer, unhappy in married life, and meeting with business reverses one after another, "came to the window." He looked in several directions one morning for relief, but it did not come. Some one remembered afterward meeting him in a car and recalled the distressed look which he cast upon all, but the observer himself was too busy to cross over and minister to him. In two hours after that he was found dead on his bed.

A Southern merchant lately made the following confession. He said that he was purchasing goods for his store in one of our large cities, that one bitterly cold afternoon just before dark, he was accosted near his hotel by a boy seven or eight years of age, who begged him for help, telling him that he was cold and hungry. The merchant was cold himself, in a hurry to get to his room and worried about business affairs and roughly told the lad to go away and let him alone. The boy's eyes filled with tears as he turned away without a word and passed into a side street bordering the hotel. It proved that this was his last effort.

All that evening the poor little pinched face and

blue eyes of the boy filled with tears, would come up to the mind of the man. He wished twenty times before and after he went to bed that he had helped the boy. As he heard the rush of the winter wind that night and caught the rattle of the sleet against the window, he realized how he would feel if that suffering lad on the street was his own son.

Next morning while walking through the office toward the breakfast hall, a stir and conversational buzz among the waiters and a few guests caused him to ask the reason. The reply was that a little boy had been found frozen to death under a side stairway of the hotel, and the coroner had been sent for.

With a strange sinking at the heart he went around the building with a number of gentlemen guests and there on the stone flags, partly under a small projecting porch floor, was the little boy who had begged him for help, cold in death. There was the same little, pinched, suffering face, and the same blue eyes wide open looking at him. But there was no light in them now, nor had they any tears. The lips that quivered before him just a few hours before were stilll enough now. He had been the last man the child had begged for help, and he had refused. Hungry, homeless, as he turned

out to be, and friendless, the child crept under the
stairway and froze to death. While the merchant
was in his warm bed, the lad was freezing not fifty
yards from him.

It was the yellow fever story over again. The
face had been pressed to the window, and looked
for help. Another face had seen it. The eyes of
both met. No help was given, and the first face
turned away and laid down to die.

But, as we said, there are other hungers, besides
that of the body. There are other things that people must have besides food if they would live.
Men and women die not only for lack of bread, but
for want of sympathy, friendship, appreciation.
kindness and love.

The author once knew a business man whose
life load was exceedingly heavy. In addition to
having an extravagant family to support, and trifling
relatives on both sides of the house to take care of,
he had hundreds of clerks and laborers under him,
and many interests to look after. He was continually in demand to counsel and direct, to revise
and supervise. Such a life calling for mental
self-collectedness and sound judgment and self-
restraint, naturally produced a grave, determined
and thoughtful face.

Besides this, his wife was a handsome and fascinating woman, and evidently had no love for him. Her fancy turned to younger men, and to one in especial whom her husband employed, and upon whom she showered an abundance of attentions, sitting up late to let him in the front door at night, and preparing dainty little dishes to tempt his appetite. The husband, who had been the benefactor of the young man, and whose money provided a luxurious home for all, was as completely neglected and ignored by his wife as though he was an outsider, and the youth with whom she was infatuated was the head of the household.

Of course the husband saw and felt it all; but he never deviated in his courtly treatment of his wife, and never uttered a word of complaint to a living creature. But such a burden did not serve to soften the lines and lighten the lineaments of an already grave and melancholy countenance.

In the last few years of his life he suffered unspeakable agony from a peculiar lung trouble. We have seen his face become in a few moments drawn with pain, and colorless as marble; and we have seen him prostrated with his physical suffering in his office or room, while his wife was taking a drive in her carriage, or sitting in the parlor or dining-room entertaining the youth already mentioned.

The face of this business man finally became a marvel to the writer in its lines of moral strength and self-mastery. He was not a Christian, did not know the Savior, was a man of the world ; and yet in his self control he was showing himself greater than he that taketh a city, and putting to shame many who were in pew and in pulpit.

Several times the life cares and business burdens and heart sorrows seemed to get the best of him, and suddenly we saw the anguished soul of the man looking out of the dark, tortured eyes. If a human figure had appeared in them, wringing its hands and crying for mercy, the vision would not have been more startling and moving than the agonized look which he turned upon us. Once we saw him cast it upon his wife. She did not see the look as she was laughing at the time over her own awkward effort to smoke a cigarette, which had been lighted and handed her by a gentleman. In another instant the face was composed again, and a few minutes later he uttered a courtly good evening, walked unattended by his wife to the hall, put on his overcoat unassisted, and, opening the door, walked away unnoticed down the darkened street to his city office where three hours hard work awaited him.

It was not long after this that he died.

In a word, the face was seen for a moment at the window. It looked in vain for help, and then turning silently away, the man laid down to die.

VII.

A CONFERENCE DIS—APPOINTMENT.

A YOUNG preacher, burning up with zeal, told the Lord in prayer just before the annual session of his conference, to send him wherever there was an abundance of work to be done. Incidentally he had learned that a certain prominent church, in one of the largest towns in his State, wanted him as pastor. Naturally he put the two facts together, and concluded that God would send him to that aforesaid large, bustling city. According to the fitness of things, he evidently should be appointed there. Why not? Here was a great church needing his consecrated activity, and here he was with his zeal, more than willing to go. The two conditions in a manner supplemented each other. It would be strange if everybody did not see it, and people did not rise up and demand it. Even now, before conference, he could almost feel the eyes of that assembly, together with the gaze of its presiding officer, turned in his direction as upon the hope of that part of Zion, and the visible solution of an ecclesiastical problem.

When, on the second day of the conference, he was informed that two telegrams had been sent to the Bishop and Cabinet, asking that he might be appointed to Swellville, where the large church in question was located, he more than ever supposed that would be his future field. He was a preacher who never requested an appointment, and never elbowed or button-holed presiding elder or lay-man on the subject. Still these outside occur-rences coming to his ears, and his own desire for increased labor, unconsciously prepared him to ex-pect that thriving city of Swellville for his next work, as the lips involuntarily pucker for a sugar plum.

To his astonishment, when the appointments were read out, he was sent to a town that was con-sidered the most broken down station in all the list. The congregation it is said was large, but it had been divided by church quarrels, neglected by previous pastors, and the house of worship was almost empty on the Sabbath.

The preacher, concerning whom this chapter is written, was almost knocked breathless as he heard his name connected for the next twelve months with the ruinous fold and scattered flock at Blank-town. He looked and felt very much as the name of the town indicated. He could scarcely credit his ears. Surely there must be some mistake. Did not the church at Swellville want him? Had not telegrams been dispatched about the matter? Undoubtedly there was a mistake.

But no, there was no blunder. The large hall still echoed with the word Blanktown! and his own name coupled with it. Then the Bishop read on as if everything was right, and no error had been made in the reading.

The balloon did not ascend that evening according to expectation. Some one had punctured it. Even now it was going down rapidly. Behold he had come to hear the appointments read that night, with his hopes spread out like the famous seven-tailed comet of long ago, and now those seven tails had folded into one, and that one had the curious drooping curve of the comet of 1859. The single hope now left was to escape from the crowd without his grief and disappointment being seen.

He thought of his distant, expectant family. How could he face that loving group which had prophesied a great promotion for him. He thought of the kind household that had entertained him during the conference session, and said they knew he would get the best appointment on the list. How could he meet them with all the fiery tails of the comet gone, and nothing but the head left, for by this time even the hope of escaping from the crowd unnoticed had departed. The blazing seven-tailed miracle of the ecclesiastical skies had been reduced and shorn and stripped until now it was twinkling just above the horizon, a star of the smallest magnitude and willing to change places with a glow-worm.

Mortified with, and disappointed in himself, the man looked with dull, dazed eyes over a sea of heads around him, and called in vain on his faint-ing, sinking, suffering heart to arouse and be true and faithful to Christ.

As soon as he could at the close of the services, and while others were shaking hands, laughing and talking, congratulating each other and saying goodbye, he took advantage of the confusion, slip-ped out and sped away through the night.

He found it a relief to run. He reached the place of his entertainment ahead of the family. For this he was thankful. Leaving words of farewell with the servant for the household, he, with valise in one hand and umbrella in the other, dashed out of the gate and ran again. This time the race course was nearly a mile. It was a

luxury to run.   He distributed a number of **groans**
upon the night air as he sped along the empty
streets.   Ambition had received a fearful stab.
Pride had met a stunning blow.   Something was
hurt in inner realms.   All that was left to do was
to exert vigorously and steadily the outside, and
thus take off some of the pressure and misery on
the inside.   The physical was called upon to relieve
the mental and spiritual.

Reaching the train, the modern Jonah took a
seat in the corner of the car where he would not
be observed, and drawing his overcoat up so as to
mantle his face, looked through the window of the
flying train upon the still night, and at the distant
stars, and fought silently with the inward misery.

By and by a voice seemed to whisper to him,
"Did you not ask God to send you where there
was abundance of work to do?"

"Yes."

"Did you not say in your prayer that it mattered not how much and how difficult the work
was?"

"Yes."

"Well, have you not obtained what you prayed
for?"

A long silence, and then the mental response—

" Yes, Lord, but I thought it would be Swellville?"

" But did you not say in your prayer that you left all that to me?"

" Yes, Lord." This time very humbly.

" Did you not ask for hard work and plenty of it, for my sake?"

" Yes, my Savior." And the eyes were wet and the heart all softened.

" Has it not come to you as you prayed?"

" Yes, Jesus."

" What will you do about it?"

" I will go, Lord."

And then there was a sudden gush of happy tears in the dark corner. The night air seemed filled with balm. The temporarily interrupted friendship with the stars was renewed, and they seemed to smile upon him from their great, tranquil depths, and to say,

" It is only a little while you have to suffer for Him, and then you will reign with Him forever."

VIII.

MR. BROWN AND MR. BRAUN.

I WAS leaving a large city to live in one still larger. Among the callers and visitors who came to see me, for various reasons, before I left, was a lady dressed in deep black and accompanied by her daughter, a girl of sixteen.

The lady who appeared to be between thirty and forty years of age was not uncomely, but had naturally a melancholy face, and an equally melancholy voice. After sundry conversational preliminaries she told me that she understood I was going to move to the large city already referred to, and though a stranger she made bold to request a great favor at my hands. She said that her husband four years before had taken their little boy and gone into business in that same city; that at first he had written regularly, then irregularly, but now for months he had ceased to correspond with them at home at all. That every kind of written appeal was ignored by him, though he was still in that city, and the letters evidently reached him, for they would otherwise have been returned by the postoffice authorities. Her request of me was to call upon him as soon as I could after my arrival and use my influence to get his consent to come back home to his wife and daughter. The address she gave me was Mr. Brown, manager of some chemical works, located on the river side in the southern part of the city.

Under the impulse of the moment, and full of sympathy for the sorrowful woman before me, I promised to pay the visit and deliver the exhortation. After she left, and especially after I arrived in the aforesaid city the magnitude and delicacy of the task grew upon me. I became sorry that I had promised. Who was I, that I could straighten a domestic affair where the two most interested had failed. And when did a man ever come out satisfactorily to himself where he meddled in the private matters of husband and wife.

The more I thought about it, the less inclined I felt to seeing Mr. Brown, and so the days slipped by through repeated postponements of the visit. At last came a letter from Mrs. Brown, asking me if I had forgotten my promise, and urging me to go at once.

One morning, a week after the arrival of the letter, I girded up my resolution, summoned what brass I could for the occasion, and took the street cars for the distant part of the city where the factory was located in which Mr. Brown was a trusted officer.

On the cars I asked the conductor if he knew of any large chemical works on the southern side of the city? He said he did, and that he went very near the place. Then would he have the goodness to put me off as near the place as he could? Yes, he would.

In due time he stopped the car at a corner, and pointed out some large buildings on the river side, a couple of blocks away, as the place desired.

Accosting a policeman on the street, I asked if he knew the name of the manager or superintendent of the chemical works just before us. He replied that he thought his name was Brown.

Without more ado, I pushed down the road which descended steeply toward the river, turned the shoulder of a great bank or bluff and crossed a long, narrow bridge, one hundred feet in length, and that ended on a line with the second story of the building. Tapping at the door I was admitted by a nice looking clerk into a cozy, well-furnished office, with revolving chairs and business desks, green-shaded electric lights, etc.

With considerable uneasiness of speech, and some nervousness of manner, I said :

" Is Mr. Brown in ? "

" Yes sir, he is in the main building, but he will be back in the office in a few moments. Be seated, sir."

I sank into a seat feeling a little weak about the knees, and first crossing and then uncrossing the lower limbs, sighed like a grampus, studied the bronze clock which ticked loudly on the mantel, moistened my lips, and made several dry swallows.

In a few moments a well-groomed business man in middle life came through an inner door into the office. With a swift glance I took in the respectable figure, the well-fitting suit of gray, the spotless linen, the Burnside whiskers, and thought " I am certainly in for it."

Taking his desk chair, and turning upon me he said in the quick tones peculiar to very busy men.

" What can I do for you, sir? "

Glancing around and seeing that the clerk was out I said.

" I suppose you are Mr. Brown? "

" Yes, sir."

" Mr. Brown, my errand is a very disagreeable one."

Here I paused while the gentleman himself looked very gravely and coldly upon me.

"Mr. Brown," I continued, swallowing quite a lump in my throat, and now determined to get through the distasteful business expeditiously—"Mr. Brown I have come to beg you to return to your wife in New Orleans."

If Mr. Brown appeared expectant before, he looked astounded now. He seemed under strong emotion and unable to reply. All of which looked very much like conscious and overtaken guilt. For a full moment he sat gazing fixedly at me, and then almost gasped:

"What did you say, sir!"

"I said, Mr. Brown, that I have come to beg you to return to your wife in New Orleans. I do this at her own request."

Mr. Brown's face at this moment looked as if he was close to a case of apoplexy, while his eyes assumed a bulging appearance. At last he fairly blurted out the words:

"What do you mean, sir? I've got no wife in New Orleans. I have never been in New Orleans in my life!"

"Isn't your name Brown?"

"My name is Braun."

"Braun?" I asked, with a great misgiving in my heart.

"Yes, sir—Braun."

"I thought the policeman and the clerk said your name was Brown?"

"I don't care what you thought sir—I know my name is Braun!"

At this moment I was fervently wishing that a subterranean passage might open beneath my chair, that I might suddenly vanish from view and be seen no more in those parts.

How I got away I can hardly tell, except I remember that I said "I was sorry" and "that I had made an unfortunate mistake," etc., and so I stammered, and sidled and backed out of the office leaving Mr. Braun standing in the middle of the floor and looking like he did not know whether to laugh or get mad, or have me arrested as an escaped lunatic.

How long that narrow bridge was that morning! Long before, it seemed endless now. As I walked along its interminable length I had a dreadful sensation that a number of curious and amused eyes were watching me from the office window. A hasty glance backward over the shoulder proved that the suspicion was true, several faces were there and all were laughing.

At last, after two minutes of time and a century of feeling, I stepped off the end of the bridge, and as I turned the bluff, putting thereby fifty feet of solid earth between me and their faces, I took the first easy breath I had drawn in the last fifteen minutes.

Going up on a business street I stepped into a large drug store and asked the owner several questions.

Have you more than one chemical factory in this part of the city?"

"Yes, sir," was his reply, " we have two. One is close by just under the river bank there, and the other is ten or twelve blocks farther down."

"Do you know the name of the managers?"

" Yes, I deal at both places. Mr. Braun is the manager of the one by the river, and Mr. Brown is head of the one farther down town."

I asked nothing more : I was too sick at heart to put another question. I saw at once my egregious blunder. Thinking there was but one chemical factory, and misled by the similarity in pronunciation of the names, Braun and Brown, I had made the distressing mistake just described.

I was in no mood to visit any more chemical works, and although the druggist kindly offered to give me the clearest directions, so that I could not miss the other and more distant one, yet I kindly but steadily refused all proffered assistance.

No, I wanted no more Browns. The one I wanted had turned out to be Braun, and who could tell but the second might prove to be Bone and Muscle, and that manifested in a remarkable and painful way.

No, I had enough of it, and so turned my face back toward the great smoky city, sadder and wiser, and determined from the bottom of my heart that from that time I would have nothing to do with chemical works, and parted husbands and wives. No, indeed; no more chemicals and no more Browns for me. As for women who had lost their husbands, let them find the domestic wanderers themselves. They caught them once before, let them do so again. Then the absurdity, if not the cruelty, of asking a busy man to find a person by the name of Brown in a city of nearly a million inhabitants, and where there were certainly a hundred Browns at the slightest computation. No, sir, or rather, no, madam, I resign to-day, with all its honors and dishonors, the high and responsible

office of husband hunter for forsaken wives.   Some
doubtless have gifts in that direction, but from bitter experience I am convinced that such a work is
not my mission, and that in a word, it is not my
forte.

*   *   *   *   *

A copy of the letter sent down the railroad to
one of the interested parties is necessary for the
proper concluding of this remarkable piece of history.

MRS. BROWN—Dear Madam :

I have endeavored to find your husband and succeeded only in a measure.   The man I visited
turned out not to be your husband.   The other
man is your husband.

I do not know that I make myself altogether
clear in this matter, but the fact is that I have gotten badly mixed up in the whole affair.

I am convinced it would be best for you to come
on.   You certainly could not make a worse failure
than I have made.

With regards and regrets, I am,

Respectfully yours,   *   *

Here endeth one of the lessons of life.

IX.

THERE had been protracted services in the church for a number of days and nights. One evening after the main audience had been dismissed, quite a number of the workers remained to labor with some penitents who were left at the altar.

One of them was a heavy set, beetle-browed man, who groaned in the most pitiful manner. Clutching our hand as we went to talk to him, he said that he felt he must partake of the Lord's Supper before he could ever gain peace of mind.

We replied that he should have it on the morrow, for it was now too late to obtain the elements.

But the man with awful groans said he could not endure the mental burden that long, for it was a case of conscience and conviction of duty with him, and that something told him if he could partake of the sacrament he would find rest and spiritual deliverance.

The news of the case soon spread through the room and quite a body of sympathetic religious people gathered about us.

Determining, late as it was, to do our utmost to

bring relief to a tortured spirit, the writer sent off to a neighboring church member for a piece of bread, and to a drug store for a bottle of wine.

The communion table was brought forth and covered with spotless damask. The silver plate was next covered with the white bread, and a large silver goblet filled with the aromatic port wine. A number of my people knelt solemnly around the altar while we read the Ritual, concluding now to make a service for all, and so a blessing to all.

With tender heart and impressive voice we broke the bread and distributed it among the kneeling figures, commencing of course with our groaning friend. We observed, however, as we passed the plate to him, that he took the tiniest crumb, and in the most careless manner placed it in his mouth. Moreover, he still groaned.

As we approached him a few moments later with the cup, which in view of a number of communicants, we had filled to the brim, the man's groanings ceased, and with unmistakable interest in this part of the service, he sat up, took the large goblet from my hand and began drinking. After a half dozen swallows he stopped a moment reflectively, seemed to approve the quality of the wine, and began to drink again.

Meantime my silence, and the stopping of the service caused numbers of the people to raise their heads. Great was the astonishment, conflicting the emotions, and varied the facial expressions of the kneeling, gazing group as they saw our groaner, groaning no longer, but with head tilted back, and the bottom of the cup pointing to the ceiling taking down the last drop of wine in the chalice. He disposed of the whole cup.

It was curious to observe the different faces of the people. Some were indignant, especially the ladies, and plainly showed it. Others were unable to credit their senses and stared with amazement at the offender and one another. Still others were shaking with laughter, while most of the men wore an expression which read as distinctly as print: " Sold again."

The custom of the Roman Catholic Church in withholding the wine while giving the bread to communicants, had been repeated in the heart of Protestantism, or evangelical Christianity ; though in our case it was forced upon us, there being nothing but bread to offer the others, inasmuch as our friend with the conscientious scruples had made away with all the wine.

Most of us did not tarry to say good-bye to our

latest convert, but each man departed to his own house, carrying a considerable amount more of light and knowledge than had been expected in the earlier part of the evening.

One brother however, approached our convert as he was departing from the church, and asked him how he felt now since he had relieved his conscience? and the man clearing his throat and wiping his mouth with the back of his hand said,

"I feel a world better."

X.

D R. KAY was the pastor of the leading church of his denomination in a large city. Afterward, he was, in recognition of his ability, made a Bishop. One Sabbath morning while filling his pulpit, his eyes fell upon a face in the audience which quite attracted him. It was the countenance of a man fully sixty years of age. The type was English, the expression open and smiling and the general appearance benevolent and patriarchal. Moreover he seemed very much impressed with the discourse.

After the sermon, the gentleman approached and was introduced to the preacher who became more interested in him as he took note of the guileless face and child-like nature of the man.

On inquiry, it turned out that he was on his way from England to visit a daughter of his who lived deep in the interior of Missouri. The funds of the old gentleman had given out in New Orleans, and here he was fifteen hundred miles by water from his daughter's home, and yet cheerful as a bob-o-link in spring time.

The preacher asked him how he proposed covering this distance in such a specieless condition. The smiling reply was that he did not know, that all he owned in the world was a copy of Mr. Wesley's magazine, printed in 1789.

The preacher told him he hardly thought he could ride to Missouri on that publication. And so being filled with a deep interest and pity for the stranger, the man of God bustled around and raised a purse from his members sufficient to pay the needed fare to the distant Western State.

The unaffected gratitude of the sunny-natured old Englishman was most pleasing. He thanked the preacher again and again, and begged him to accept as a token of his gratitude, Mr. Wesley's magazine, printed in 1789. The preacher with smiles refused the valuable remuneration, and told him he would not deprive him of such a treasure.

In due time the steamer swung out into the Mississippi and disappeared around the Carrolton curve, carrying the cheerful hearted old Englishman.

Six months rolled away, and not a word had been heard from him, when suddenly one Sabbath morning, as Dr. Kay was in the midst of his discourse, he glanced down and saw the face of the sunny faced Briton shining at him, just as though he had never left the pew since last seen, and had never been to Missouri. The greeting after the sermon was of the same cordial, open character that had distinguished the first. The returned traveler seemed unaffectedly glad to see the preacher, and the preacher could not for his life keep back a warm smile and cordial hand-shake from the little old man who was so persistently sunny and winning.

Of course the question came plump out from the preacher:

"What on earth are you doing here! I thought you were a thousand miles away in the northwest."

"So I was," replied the Briton, "but I had not been long with my daughter, when I saw my son-in-law did not want me. My welcome wore out in a month's time, and I felt that I must go back to England."

"How did you manage to get here?" asked the preacher. "Did your daughter or son-in-law help you financially?"

"O no, not a cent. I just got on a steamboat on the Missouri river and came here."

"Did they let you travel free?" asked the preacher.

"Well, they had to ; there was no other way for me to travel. What did I have ! So just as soon as the boat went to puffing down the river the clerk came to me and asked me for my fare. I told him I had nothing in the world to give him except a copy of Mr. Wesley's Magazine, printed in the year 1789. And what do you suppose the clerk did?" And the smiling old man grew grave and pensive for a few moments.

"I am afraid to guess," replied the preacher. "Well, sir," said the Briton, "I'll tell you. He cussed Mr. Wesley, and cussed the magazine, and turned around and cussed me."

The preacher bowed his head quickly to hide a smile, which in spite of every effort would overspread itself in boldest lines and curves upon the face.

"Yes, sir," resumed the grieved little man, "he cussed us all."

"Did he let you stay on the boat after that?" inquired the minister.

"Yes. He never paid any more attention to me all the way down to New Orleans."

"How do you propose getting back to England, if you are without money?"

"I have a son in Canada near Quebec," replied

the old gentleman. "If I could get to him, I could manage the rest of the trip back home, some way, through him."

After saying this all care seemed to leave the speaker, and his accustomed serenity and sunniness of spirit returned with an actual gathered force.

It all resulted as before in Dr. Kay taking up a second private collection, during the week. And so there was a second surprise for the simple-minded old gentleman, and a second outpouring of thanks on his part. But in another second he added,

" I would be so glad if you would accept as a token of my gratitude for all your kindness, a copy of Mr. Wesley's magazine printed in the year 1789. It is the only one that I have, and it is all that I have."

The preacher however graciously and steadily refused, though Mr. Wesley's admirer for the space of several minutes continued to urge him to accept the wonderful publication.

A few days afterward, the old gentleman betook himself with his beaming smiles and sunny nature to the train on his way to Canada.

Twelve months rolled by, and the remembrance of the individual had dropped from Dr. Kay's mind, when he received a letter through the mail with the postmark of a town in England upon the envelope. It proved to be from Mr. Wesley's admirer. He said that he had safely reached his son's home in the Dominion, spent a number of months very pleasantly with him, and had finally left for England. He had just arrived a few days before, safe and sound, after an absence of two years. He furthermore related that he could not but be grateful to the preacher in America who had been so kind to him, and as a token of his affectionate regard would be glad to send him a copy of Mr. Wesley's magazine, printed in the year 1789, but he feared if the volume should be sent by mail it would not reach him. Meantime he begged to remain as ever, his obliged humble servant, etc., etc.

This was the end of the personal history of the English gentleman as known on this side of the water ; but the whole occurrence itself was a marvelous illustration of the privileges and possibilities of the Nineteenth century. The bit of biography narrated in this chapter establishes as perfectly true and reasonable the amazing occurrences of a certain book called ''The Arabian Nights :'' and even shows that they can be surpassed. In that famous volume we read that a Prince would put a small carpet the size of a rug on the ground, place him-

self upon the limited area, and immediately be
borne away to distant parts of the earth. But here
an old gentleman, not a prince, takes a copy of Mr.
Wesley's magazine, printed in the year 1789, and
rides, so to speak, upon it from England to America, from New Orleans to Missouri, from the far-
away west back to the Gulf of Mexico, from Louis-
iana to Canada, and from Canada back to England.

In all these trips the man sees many wonderful
things, makes delightful acquaintances, visits his
daughter in the west and his son in the east, and after
years of such traveling, visiting, eating, drinking
and sleeping, returns home without the journey having cost him personally a single cent; the whole
thing having been accomplished by a copy of Mr.
Wesley's magazine, printed in the year 1789.

It might however, be well to say, that not every
one could ride the book that far. That to make the
wonderful recorded trip or ride as given in this chapter there was required, in addition to the magazine,
a certain compound of smiles, sunniness of manner,
and child-like innocence upon the part of the rider
himself.

Nevertheless all can see that the book really
carried the rider.

XI.

A NIGHT ADVENTURE.

THERE had been a number of missionary addresses delivered by prominent ministers and laymen. A collection had been taken up with the usual auctioneering feature, "who will give five dollars?" the regulation sending out of painfully self-conscious brethren with hats as collection baskets, and the customary exchange of ancient and threadbare witticisms between the collectors and the brother in charge of the collection, as he stood in his directing capacity on the platform.

The congregation had been trickling out for an hour and so at the singing of the doxology there were hardly one hundred people left. With the pronouncing of the benediction this remainder speedily passed out on the street and was swallowed up in the shadows of the streets.

The treasurer and the chairman of the missionary board, in the counting up of the cash and straightening certain accounts, were the only persons left in the building, with the exception of the sexton, who waited sleepily and anxiously near the door for their departure, that he might shut up the church and go home.

The first mentioned officer had been carrying around with him for days a black tin box, about a foot square, containing over a thousand dollars of the conference missionary money. To this was added a thousand more that night; and now, with a feeling of great relief he turned it all over to the chairman, and bidding him good night, walked out of the front door of the church, while the other two retired through a rear entrance.

As the large, heavy doors closed behind the treasurer, he found that the street in which he stood was pitch dark, while the town clock from the distant court house belfry was striking the hour of eleven.

He almost felt his way across to the opposite pavement, had placed his foot on the brick walk, when out of a shadowy recess or alley way, somewhat to his left, a voice said :

" Good evening."

Very promptly the treasurer replied, " Good evening," but unable to see the form, and feeling that no one with right intentions should be addressing him at such a time, he turned to the right and walked on his way up the pavement.

To his exceeding discomfort he saw in a mo-that he was being followed, and as the tread of the pursuing footsteps sounded close behind, the voice spoke again.

"Excuse me, sir, but who preached to-night?"

Looking backward the treasurer saw the form of the man, but could not see his face. He replied:

"No one preached, sir; we had a number of missionary addresses."

In another moment the man had reached his side, and looking up the treasurer discovered to his horror that the man's face was covered with a black mask.

At once it flashed upon him that the man had spotted him during the preceding days as he had walked to and from the church with the missionary cash box in his hand, and now knowing that there had been an additional collection, had determined to waylay the cash bearer and rob him.

With the thought came at the same time the realization of his own helplessness. The streets were dark and forsaken, the people of the town all home by this time in bed, while the man who walked by his side was both taller and heavier. Moreover, he could not tell at what time the masked man would strike or shoot him down.

There was a single light twinkling in a residence, the gallery of which came down to the edge

of the brick walk. The first impulse of the treasurer was to step quickly on the porch, ring the
bell, and ask to remain there for the night, as he
knew the family. But a second thought came up,
why be alarmed so soon? and one should be ashamed
to run before a single attack has been made upon
him. So the house was passed, and the two walked
farther up the dark avenue together.

As they reached the next corner, the preacher
looked down the street on the left hand which led
south. With the exception of a single light gleaming through a door or window in the distance, the
whole street was black. Two blocks away a large
wooden bridge spanned a deep railroad cut, and
beyond that were some empty lots with a few scattering houses which lay between the bridge and
the suburban house where the subject of this
narrative was entertained. Darkness lay over
it all.

Of course it was evident now to the mind of the
preacher that the plan of the robber was to accom-
pany him beyond the bridge, and somewhere on
the road among the lonely lots, shoot, or strike him
down, and make off with the box of money which
he believed his victim still had in charge.

The treasurer hesitated a moment at the corner,

scarcely knowing what to do, when the masked man asked :

" Which way are you going?"

" I shall take this street toward the bridge," was the answer, with the hope that the unwelcome companion would say that he intended going straight on. Instead, he replied :

" I'll go along with you."

And so he did, walking silently by his side. As they proceeded down the street together, thought was busy in the mind of the preacher as to what was best to be done. There was no sign of a watchman, and everybody seemed to have gone to bed. What could be done !

Suddenly he conceived a plan, and acted upon it. They were nearing the solitary light which issued from an open door and fell a narrow path of brightness on the pavement before them. He felt that if he passed that border of radiance and went out into the shadowy and forsaken streets beyond the bridge he would be murdered, and no one ever be the wiser as to how and by whom it was done. If he was knocked down and robbed of the two hundred dollars in his pocket which the chairman of the board had given him to present to one of the conference missionaries at the house where he was staying, many would not believe in his story, and he would have a cloud to rest upon him all the rest of his life.

So just as they got opposite the door, the preacher, without a moment's hesitation, suddenly turned and walked through it into the building and left his companion evidently astonished at the unexpected movement on the street.

The place proved to be several things in one. On the left side was a fancy grocery store, on the right curtained stalls for eating, while a bar-room with green blinds was in the rear. Not a soul was in front, but voices could be heard from behind the screen in the saloon. The air was impregnated with whisky, and the thick and stammering language of the unseen speakers, showed unmistakably that the owners thereof were well on the way to intoxication, if not already there.

At this moment the man on the street entered, and the mask was still on his face. Stepping up to the preacher he asked in a voice trembling with anger, " What do you mean by coming in here,"

The minister said quietly but firmly,

" I came in to get rid of you. You annoy me." As he said this he threw his cloak back over his shoulders so that though still buttoned at the neck it hung down his back. This was done carelessly,

but also designedly, that the man might see that the
tin box was not on hand. And this he did see,
and the recognition was evident to the preacher in
spite of the mask.

By this time the owner of the store hearing
voices in front, came forward attended by two men
who were evidently far gone in liquor. As the
young preacher looked on the coarse, bestial face
of the saloon-keeper, took note of the two drunken
men, and then his eye fell again upon the masked
man, who strange to say did not leave, and did not
unmask, his heart sank at the thought of his sur-
roundings and company at such an hour and so far
from any friend or earthly assistance. He felt as
he looked at them all that he could expect no help
from any one of them.

One additional fact that made his heart sink still
lower, was that he saw a swift glance of recognition or intelligence of some kind pass between the
masked man and the others. Not a syllable of
surprise was uttered by one of the three that a fourth
man had on a black mask which only allowed his
eyes to be seen.

The saloon-keeper turned to the preacher and
said shortly,

" What will you have?"

His reply was,

" I came in here to get rid of this man, who persists in following me."

In answer to this the man with the face covering whirled upon the speaker and gave him a fearful cursing. Dreadful as it was, there was nothing to do but to take it.

Finally the man exhausted his fury and profane vocabulary, and concluded with the words that the preacher might go home, or to the bottom of the pit for what he cared, that he did not want anything to do with him one way or the other.

The preacher endured the abuse trying as it was, being shrewd enough to see that it was a venting of spleen and a covering up of the would be thief's disappointment at the absence of the tin box.

So feeling that it was not more dangerous to go than to remain in such a place, he walked out of the store and with a rapid step struck out for the railroad bridge. He fully expected to be followed, and had the curious sensation in the back and along the spinal cord that some one was pursuing him and ready to strike or stab him.

When he gained the bridge he glanced back, but could see no one. Even the light had disappeared by the closing of the door, or by having been extinguished.

He crossed the bridge, and entered the gloomy, empty lots, and walked swiftly along the sparsely settled road with its few houses standing back in their yards, while the sensation still played like invisible fingers on the nerves, testifying by a language of touches that some one was following closely in the dark.

At last, after having trudged a distance of nearly a half dozen blocks, the preacher reached the gate, entered the yard, and stood on the gallery of the house owned by his host. By the light streaming out of the transom, and voices inside, he knew that the family and other ministerial guests had not retired. Never did light look more beautiful, nor voices sound sweeter.

He rapped on the door, and was not heard at first because of the hum of conversation. The creeping sensation in the backbone testified to unpassed danger, and the nervous glance of the eye backward revealed a dark object moving near the gate. Again the preacher knocked, and this time louder. Some one approached from within, the door opened, and the hunted man stepped in from the dark, chilly night, into the warm, bright room filled with loving friends while a cheerful fire crackled on the hearth. Never did lamp and fire look brighter and people appear more attractive and delightful.

A great black mantle of anxiety and even dread slipped from off his shoulders on the gallery, the door was closed upon it, and the preacher sat down with the family and guests in comfort and safety, with such a feeling of mental relief, gladness of heart, and gratitude to God for divine protection and deliverance, that no words could possibly describe.

After a few minutes the strange occurrences of the night were related to the group, who had purposely sat up waiting for the arrival of the preacher and were wondering at his long delay.

While he told the history of the night, a deep silence fell upon all ; and when the conclusion was reached. the unanimous conviction and expressed opinion was that God had delivered his servant from a deadly peril.

XII.

A PASTORAL ROUND.

THE church to which a certain preacher was appointed by the conference was languishing and
even dying for pastoral work. It had been favored
with gifted men, with scholars and orators, but
these brethren had preferred their studies and libra-
ries, with pen and pencil, to the house-to-house visiting that was needed.

Then there had been one or two ministers who
were neither preachers nor pastors, so the charge
had gone steadily down, and a corporal's guard of
an audience remained where once had been a large
congregation.

The new preacher found this to be the state of
things on his arrival, and also discovered that two-
thirds of the membership lived in the country from
one to seven miles. To cap the climax, the rem-
nant or faithful few left in town were financially
unable to provide him with horse or vehicle to
hunt up the missing and absent ones.

He lost no time in fruitless regrets and com-
plaints. His heart burned to see the work of God

revive, and a great tenderness filled his breast for the wandering sheep of the fold. He determined to go after them, and to do it on foot. The people must be gotten back to the house of God, and to Christ.

His first walk over fields, through **woodlands**, and along country lanes, extended from the suburbs to quite a number of miles as he pushed farther and farther, with each trip, to reach the people who had left the church, forgotten duty, and were going farther astray all the time as the years went by. If they would not come to him, he would go to them. And he did.

One day he started out on one of his rounds. It was a cold afternoon, with a bleak wind cutting his face and occasional flurries of snow filling the air. He visited from house to house beyond the corporation lines, getting farther and farther from town, while the roads became white with the increasing snow, the dusk settled upon the landscape, and the distant lights of the town glimmered faintly over the darkening fields.

He spent a half an hour with each family, engaged in kindly talk about their temporal welfare, then passed into spiritual conversation, concluding the visit with a brief passage from the Scriptures and a tender, unctuous prayer in the midst of the family, who knelt around him. Arising from his knees with his eyes wet, he would find the eyes of the others moistened like his own, and sometimes with faces bathed with tears.

A number of visits had thus been paid when the black night found him several miles from town, knocking at the door of still another house. It was the home of a local preacher who had become hurt and soured over church affairs and was now absenting himself from any and all meetings. When in response to the knock he opened the door and saw his new preacher standing on the threshold, with a black night and heavy snow storm for a background, he was astounded and could scarcely utter the words which, as they came from his lips, were spoken as if a full period came after each.

"W h y—what—on—earth—brings—you—out such—a—night—as—this?"

The simple response of the preacher was,

"I am after my Lord's sheep."

There was that in the quiet, loving answer that went like an arrow to the local preacher's heart, for with dimmed eyes and broken voice he put his arm around the visitor, drew rather than led him into the

room, and placed him in an easy chair before a great
cheery fire that was blazing up the chimney.

It was a large family circle and all seemed
strangely touched and drawn to the man of God
who had come to see them through such weather,
and not only that, but to spend the night. He walked
right into every one of their hearts that evening,
even before the time for family prayer. The singing of the old time Methodist hymns in the fire-
side worship sounded in sweet contrast to the rushing storm outside. All were remembered by name
in the prayer that followed, and heaven came very
near. They all felt shut in with God, and the
hard lines that had been gathering on the local
preacher's face for several years back were all
wiped out that night.

Next morning, when he stood with his family on
the porch, saying goodbye to their pastor, who intended pushing on still farther in the country after
the scattered sheep of his flock, there was a look in
his face that had not been there for many months.
Waving his hand to the departing preacher, he cried
out,

"We will all be in to church next Sunday, rain
or shine."

The preacher smiled back at the group, and was

not a whit surprised at the promise. He had seen real pastoral medicine tried before and he felt in his soul that Christ had this family in his love and grasp again.

The snow had ceased falling and now lay deep everywhere. The clouds lay in thick, ashen gray bands over the sky, and the wind, now veered into the north, was so keen and bitter that not a human being could be seen in field or upon the road.

This state of things, however, was in agreement with and for the furtherance of his plans. He wanted to see the men as well as the women and children of his flock. And now he knew he would find them all housed, for the snow was too deep and the weather too severe for them to do any outside work. And he so found them.

He trudged across the white frozen fields all day, breaking through the icy crust, knocking off the snow in fleecy showers from the fences he climbed, opening ice-clad gates, and astonishing many families by his unexpected appearance on foot and alone, but leaving them later all drawn to him, and better still to his Saviour, by his evident interest in and love for them. His closing prayer, in which he often individualized each member of the family, pleading for their happiness, usefulness, prosperity and salvation, invariably melted them, and almost without exception left the entire family in tears.

Women with a baby in arms and smaller tots hanging on to their dress stood in the door with a pleased smile and asked him to come again. The shamefaced father or husband would at times follow him to the gate or bars, chewing a pine splinter, and looking like he wanted to get something off his mind and heart, but did not know which end of the matter to take hold of for the verbal lift. Observing the embarrassing silence, the preacher took the large brown hand in his and said just as he was leaving.

"I hope I will see you at church next Sunday?" When the reply came like a pistol shot,

"I'll be there."

And he was.

At the hour of sunset the preacher found himself seven miles from home in the heart of a great pine forest. The snow lay outspread around him like a vast white carpet, the trunks of the great pines shot up in the air over an hundred feet high, while every leaf was encased in glittering ice. The tree trunks looked like the pillars of a majestic temple, and the wind sighing through their tops flung down upon him from this natural æolian harp the sweetest and yet most weird of music. Just then there was a rift in a cloud in the west and the sunlight dashed for a few minutes through the grove and fairly transfigured the spot, beautiful as it was before. The tree tops had become a roof of diamonds and the tree trunks pillars of rosy light.

The man stood enraptured at the vision and crying out:

"Lord, what a temple of glory in which to worship Thee," he stretched himself out on the snow in prayer, praise and adoration. His heart was on fire and he scarcely felt the chill of the frozen ground with its cold covering.

Later on he stood up, drinking in the beauty and solemnity of the scene, until the light began to pale, the trees looked spectral and the sigh up in mid-air sounded more lonesome than ever.

Suddenly the thought came to him like an injected whisper:

"Who knows where you are? Who cares where you are? Others of your brethren are in easy places to-day, and here you are hunting up poor people all day, and at nightfall in the woods, tired, hungry, cold, and hardly knowing where you are and which direction to take. The very

city that asked for you has already forgotten you.
Who knows where you are, and who cares?"

The dejection lasted only a minute, for swiftly
the sweet thought seemed to be shot into the mind
and from there sank into the heart,

"Jesus knows."

An ineffable gladness at once swept into him and
a glory indescribable filled the shadowy woods.

Looking up he said, "Lord, which way shall I
go?"

He had hardly uttered this when he heard a cock
crow in the distance. Going in the direction of
the sound, he came out in ten minutes upon a field
with a house in the center containing two rooms
with an open hall connecting the two. The dwelling and little farm proved to belong to one of his
church members.

In this home he made seven new warm friends,
consisting of the father, mother, and five children.
In the country where the people hear rarely from
the outside world a visitor is always welcome, but
when he is a Christian, and one's own pastor at
that, he is doubly welcome.

The evening meal was simple, consisting of
bread, hominy, pork and milk. Grace was said and
all ate with thankful hearts. Afterward, when gath-

ered around the fire, there was a little talk about the great busy world, considerably more about the church in town, its melancholy condition, etc., and then some tender, but close conversation about what the Savior was to each one of us.

Then came the hour of family worship. The wind roared down the wide mud chimney and gusts of smoke would be driven into the room where they knelt, but there was a holy fire burning in the soul of the preacher and the smoke ascending through the grimy rafters looked to his warm heart like clouds of incense from a holy altar and like the glory that used to come down and fill God's tabernacle.

He was placed to sleep at bedtime in the room across the hall. Great cracks yawned between the logs which made the four walls of the apartment, and the cold wind swept through and over him all night, but the arms of Jesus were about him and he slept or rested as sweetly as a child in the cradle, and far more comfortably than some of earth, whose beds are of down, but whose pillows are of thorns.

The next morning, the third day out, the preacher turned his face townward and homeward, but returning by a different road.

There had come a sudden change of weather early that morning: the sun shone brightly and warmly and there was a great thaw. Through the soft snow and slush and mud he pulled his way along, going from house to house with his half-hour visits, which he invariably terminated with the Word of God and prayer. He reserved the house of a noted infidel for his last call, as a kind of dessert to the varied meal of which he had been partaking.

The man lived two miles from town, had not been to church for many years, and was given up as a hard case. The preacher knew all this, but undaunted knocked at the door at 2 o'clock in the afternoon. The man, like all the rest who had been visited, was astonished. He was surprised in the first place that a preacher should come to see him, and marvelled to behold him on foot and in such a day. He was evidently taken aback, so when he asked,

"What brings you out on such a day and so far from town?" the preacher replied, "To see you, Brother Scott." The voice was full of kindness and he had called him Brother Scott, an old, hardened, profane sinner!

The man's well-known boldness and confidence

were now all gone, and with a nervous, embarrassed air and a husky voice he asked the minister to come in. Maybe he felt the warm, loving spirit which filled his guest; perhaps the kindness and interest showed in him by walking so far to see him touched his heart. Anyhow the preacher saw with a quick glance that the lines of the man's face were softened, and so turning to him he said,

" Brother Scott, I have called on you because I love your soul and because I was once far off from God and no one came to help me."

He then with heaven-anointed tongue told the silent man how once he was living in sin, and going to ruin, that he had not been to church in years and no one seemed to care for his soul, that right in the midst of that kind of life God touched his heart and he found his soul longing for peace and pardon and yet not knowing how to get it, how he wrote to his mother about his determination to do better, and she wrote him in reply to commence praying; how he did it in ignorance and discouragement, with all kinds of difficulties in his way, and how one morning while praying, all humbled and looking to Christ, the blessing of salvation came, and God filled his soul with a blessed sense of pardon and such peace, joy and love that he cried out and wept aloud in the presence of his wife.

He had proceeded thus far when, happening to look at the infidel, he saw the tears running down his cheeks. The man seemed ashamed of his emotion and stepping quickly to the door, went out on the gallery and began to halloo loudly to some person in the field. The fact was that there was no one there, but the whole procedure was a ruse to get away from the speaker, break the strange spell that was upon him and recover his self-control in the cold, fresh air outside.

On his return from calling the imaginary individual, his face had become stone-like again. But nothing daunted, the preacher begged him to kneel down with him in prayer, and down he went, while God filled the room with His holy presence. In parting the man of God asked the infidel if he would come to church, and he said he would.

There was one more place the preacher felt like visiting before rounding up his pastoral round, and that was a large deserted camp ground, one mile from town and on still another road. So cutting across the fields, and crossing a broad, foaming branch or creek on a log, and climbing a steep hill, and then with a descent upon the other side, he came upon the empty and silent camp ground with its rows of wooden cottages and central tabernacle.

He walked along one of the streets past the closed and barred tents, and entering the great auditorium, passed down one of its steep aisles to the altar below. Here he sat a great while in the shadows of the waning afternoon, drinking in the stillness of the sacred place, recalling the scenes of glory he had beheld there and thinking of the godly people he had met, worshiped with, and rejoiced with. around this very altar.

They were all far away now. The empty benches were mutely, but painfully eloquent. The pain that comes from beholding a place alone, where one has previously been, and happy with others, was upon him. Looking up he said,

"Lord, they are all scattered and gone, but you are here. You never leave your servants," and down he went on the sawdust in the altar, face downward and at full length.

What a time he had! The camp-meeting of the year before was nothing to the glory which God poured into his soul.

He must have been there bowed in worship fully an hour. Then arising he talked to the Saviour, as one speaks to a friend, face to face. What a conversation it was! What a communion of flame! The old Tabernacle seemed to be filled with a heavenly presence and all sense of loneliness was utterly gone.

After a while he arose, went up the hill, and down the road towards town. On reaching it he learned that some one had been very sick in his absence, that the messengers had scoured the country for him in every direction, but they could not overtake him. They heard of him everywhere, but could not find him.

It was all right that they did not. The Lord did not intend that they should. He knew that the sickness was not unto death and He wanted His scattered sheep visited and fed. So God saw to it that His servant finished his pastoral round before he heard of the sickness.

The preacher had been gone three days. Many homes had been visited and hundreds of people talked and prayed with. Very gracious also were some of the fruits of that single pastoral campaign in the reclamation and salvation of souls.

One result, however, was noticed by everybody, and seen at once, and that was such a crowd at church on the following Sunday as had not been beheld since the day of its dedication. Wagons,

carriages and buggies lined the street in front and
the road that ran on the side of the church.
Horses nickered and mules brayed in chorus, while
all the benches in the meeting house were filled,
hundreds of cordial handgrasps were given, hearts
melted, eyes filled, and Arlington, Dundee and
Old Hundred were sung with an unction and volume that sent a wave of astonishment over the
neighborhood and a still bigger billow of glory up
to heaven.

Of course there were some present who did not
understand and wondered at the great gathering,
but others knew, and while receiving the bread of
life from the pastor's lips that day, had a mental
picture of a lonely black-robed figure toiling over
the fields and flitting along snow-covered roads,
with a look in his face that translated meant, "I
seek the Lord's sheep that are lost."

One brother delivered himself in the churchyard
before driving off with his family. He spoke ora-
cularly, if not originally. Waving his whip in the
air, and nodding his head to a group of church
members, he said, "It never fails, gentlemen. A
house going preacher makes a church going people." And they all said, Amen.

XIII.

THE CHILDREN.

A HOUSE without children never looks like a real home. It certainly can not be one to him who has studied the meaning of the word, and it ceases to feel like one when the little ones have grown up, gone away, or been taken to heaven.

A friend of the author had a beautiful home, but his three sons and two daughters were all grown and departed. Two of the sons and the daughters were married and lived in far distant cities, and the youngest boy of eighteen was a prodigal wandering afar off, they knew not where. The home was a luxurious one, but it was empty. The shouts, songs, voices, steps of the children had first changed in character and then died away altogether. The father, now with whitened hair, felt the loneliness keenly, but had his business cares to blunt the pain. The mother wandered restlessly through the house all day. Again and again the father found her standing before the pictures of the children as they hung upon the walls of the parlor or in the bedrooms.

One day he said to her as he thus discovered her with eyes full of tears fixed on the portrait of the absent prodigal boy :

"Wife, what are you crying about? What is the matter with you these days, wandering about the house like a ghost?"

Turning to him with trembling lips and great tears rolling down her cheeks, she replied :

"Husband, aren't the children gone?"

*   *   *   *   *   *

In a city in California where we spent a few days, we became impressed with a mansion that stood solitary and most of the time silent near where we boarded. It showed but little life and stir at any time, and never did we see a child.

Once we had occasion to go through the large yard, and passed a corner shaded with crepe myrtle trees, that had long ago been a playground for the children. We saw a small bat almost covered with the soil lying on the ground. Evidently many months had passed since the little hand had played ball with the forgotten piece of wood on the grass.

But that which most deeply touched the heart was the sight of a little grave, ten or twelve inches long, with a marble slab at the head, and on it engraved the words :

" HERE LIES BUNNIE."

The miniature tomb of the domestic pet was only a few feet from where the bat lay. Many rains had stained the one and almost buried the other. " Bunnie " had evidently died first, and his little master doubtless used to play around the tomb and remember his pet. It was pathetic to see the bat so near the grave. Then by and by the boy himself went—whether to the grave, or to some distant place to live, we could not tell—only that both were gone and both seemed now forgotten.

We walked away with a misty feeling in the eyes and a choking sensation in the throat which we had trouble with for some hours.

 * * * * * *

In a town in Florida, we overlooked from our room window at the hotel, another such stripped home as described.

The garden was filled with a profusion of southern flowers. The large back yard was beautifully shaded with great water oaks and rustling magnolias. The spring sunshine fell like a glory over it all. But there were no children to be seen. That they once had been there we found out by an affecting circumstance.

Out in the branches of one of the smaller trees

and near the flowers the servants hung a parrot in its cage every morning. Soon we noticed that he was calling the names of children. Clear and distinct over the flowers and through the trees came to our window the words, "Willie!" then, "Annie!" later on, "Charlie!" after a pause, "Minnie!"

Sometimes the bird would repeat one of the names several times before going to another, and this with the waiting after each call as if expecting an answer, at last made the sound unspeakably affecting.

The history of the case was that two of the children had died and two had been taken North to live. The household pet, who had watched them play and enjoyed their sports from his airy perch many months, had been left behind with a part of the family. But he missed the children and kept calling for them.

The servant maid scolded him at times, but it had no effect. As she went back into the house, and he was left out in the yard alone, the old calls would come pealing over the garden to our window—"Charlie!" "Minnie!" "Annie!" "Willie!" until our heart felt sick and sore.

We wondered if Charlie and Minnie away up

in the North ever recalled their pet to mind, if they were as faithful to his memory as he was to theirs.

Somehow we thought of Longfellow's poem that we have always considered a gem. One verse alone is a perfect picture:

> " The large Newfoundland house dog
> Stands watching at the door;
> He is looking for his little playmates,
> Who will return no more."

When a small lad, the writer used to follow his mother up into the large attic of our home, where trunks and many other things were stored. It was always a dark, mysterious and solemn place to him as a boy, and a certain occurrence which he beheld there more than once did not lessen at all its melancholy influence. That occurrence would be the bitter weeping of his mother over one of these open trunks. With wondering childish eyes we would creep near, hearing her sobs, and find her with a tiny little sock or shoe in her lap; or she had come across the rattle of the baby now under the sod, or find the cap or ball or some plaything of a little fellow who had been asleep under the cedars in the cemetery for twenty years.

God bless the children. How they break up our selfish lives and melt our cold hearts while with us in the world, and how they draw us after them with cords of tender power when they have slipped away into heaven.

It is marvelous how empty their going away makes the house, and indeed the world itself. And it is equally marvelous how dear and homelike heaven seems to the soul when the little ones of the househlod have gone up to walk the golden streets and live with the angels.

God grant that we may all meet the children again. We can not afford to be parted from them and see them no more.

XIV.

THE study of children is a very fascinating occupation of the mind to me. It seems to grow upon me as I become older, and I find myself often pausing in my walks to watch them trooping home from school, or gathered in merry shouting bands in the streets at play. It might be difficult to tell just why the heart gets tender and the eyes misty as we observe the eager little fellows all absorbed in their own conversation and games. What is there in the sight of those gray and brown jackets, well-worn knee pants, bundles of school books, faces flushed with exercise, and those glad resounding calls and cries, to make one's heart soften and eyes brim over?

Maybe there is a sudden vision of one's own boyhood, a swift recollection of days as bright and free from care. Or there is a boy of your own of their age far away from your presence and protection ; or there is a little fellow whose voice used to ring out like these upon the streets and in the yard, but who is now in heaven, God having taken him

from you.   Or the tenderness may come from the
thought of how much in the line of sorrow and labor
and pain awaits these romping, merry little players
on the street.   Whatever may be the cause, the interest is there, tender heart, misty eyes and all.

*   *   *   *   *   *

It does not take much to make a true, genuine
boy happy. A pocket knife and a dog satisfies many
of them thoroughly for years. The deep friendship
existing between the lad and his pet is to me one of
the most touching of spectacles. There seems to
be an understanding and a communion between
them.   I have seen the boy in trouble go to his dog
for a silent but not less real consolation.   Pretty
soon he would be seen with his arm around the
animal's neck, or his head resting upon the shaggy,
reclining body. The dog seemed to understand the
whole matter, and bent himself to the task of winning a smile from his young master.   It would not
be long before the merry peal of laughter would be
heard floating in the air, and boy and dog would be
seen going off together more than ever inseparable.

A few days since, in one of my evening rambles
about the town, I saw a lad playing ball in the side
yard of his home, while his dog lay in the grass
watching him. The boy was throwing the ball

against the side of the brick wall and catching it as
it rebounded. Two things about the scene amused
and yet touched me : one was the dog's evident interest in the game and his approval of the way his
young master was managing the whole thing, and
the second was the boy's perfect contentedness
with the companionship of the dog. He seemed to
care for no other friend or spectator.

*   *   *   *   *   *

I have often watched with deep interest two or
three little fellows standing in front of a large show
window, and in deep consultation over the mysteries therein displayed. I would gladly have given
a great deal to hear their remarks. Of course, when
it is a display of confectionery we are in no doubt
about the topic. We have frequently seen ragged
and hungry children trying to take in a satisfying
meal thus through the eyes. Once in London, about
eight years ago, I was approaching Fleet street when
I saw a little fellow standing before the show window
of a confectionery. The display of tarts, pies, cakes,
bon bons and rosy apples must have been very trying to him. The figure before me was small and
ragged, and the attitude pathetic. He was looking
and inwardly wishing, but expecting nothing. I had
just purchased a fine red apple for my own eating,

but as my eyes fell on the wistful figure before me I changed my plan. Stealing up quietiy behind the child I gently pushed the apple between his arm and body and then upward that his eyes might fall upon it. His eyes did drop, and when he saw the beautiful fruit there was first a look of astonishment, which gave way at once to one of pleasure and gratitude as he saw my smile and heard me say, "It is yours." As the little fellow sunk his teeth deep in the fruit and walked away, I felt the juice of the apple on my own palate, and I have thought and said since that the most delicious apple I ever ate was one that a little boy masticated for me years ago on the streets of London.

*   *   *   *   *   *

While I was in New England, some weeks ago, I read in the columns of one of the large dailies concerning a little boy nine years of age, living in New Mexico, who had accidentally shot and killed his little brother two years younger than himself. The unfortunate father was a minister of the gospel, and on my coming into New Mexico he had me to spend one or two days with him and his church. I saw the yard in which the accidental shot had been fired and the poor little unconscious victim picked up. The father and I took a long walk together. He showed me a tree far beyond the suburbs of the town, where the two boys, who were devoted to each other, had been praying and singing hymns together just three days before the melancholy affair took place. A quarter of a mile further, in a sandy, rock-strewn, wind-swept and treeless cemetery, I was shown the grave of the slain lad. Ascending the sides of the foot hills close by, the father and I knelt together in prayer. But my thoughts and prayer went out mainly for the living brother, who had been sent away some hundreds of miles to school.

Next day I left to hold a meeting in a town ninety miles away. The father showed his spiritual wisdom in sending for his boy to attend this meeting. So when one morning I saw the father, daughter and son walking in together, my heart swelled with emotions that would be very hard to put on paper. The very sight of the lad with his clear, manly face, the memory of the awful deed his little hands had unwittingly committed, the fear that Satan would in future years bring shadow and misery upon him, the great desire that the preaching would get hold of him and be an eternal deliverance as well as blessing to him—all these things so filled my thoughts and moved **my** heart that I began speaking with a choking utterance. Time after time as I looked at the boy, I would experience this choking sensation, while my heart continually ascended to God to bless the lad.

When I called for penitents and seekers, he was the first at the altar. In another moment his father was by his side. For four days the child came to the altar night and morning. Each time I went to him, praying with and talking to him, my arm about his form, and again and again I found him weeping ; saw he was really seeking ; and, better than this, saw him obtain what he wanted. After this, while working in the altar, I used to notice him in the corner of the church poring over his Bible. On the eighth day his sister, sixteen years old, yielded to the influence of the Word and came rushing to the altar. At once I saw him leave his seat and fall down by her side. When I reached them his sobs in her behalf were most touching to hear, as he knelt with one arm around her, while his face was buried in the other. Dear little fellow, may the Lord forever keep the shadow out of his life and make him a power for God and humanity.

*   *   *   *   *   *

Can any one explain the deep emotion felt in

listening to several hundred children singing? We have heard a thousand grown people engaged in song in a body together without any special movement of the heart, but we have never listened to a band of children sing without being profoundly affected. It matters not whether it is a national anthem, or one of the popular street songs, or some special piece for the occasion, we invariably melt as we hearken to the childish voices going up together at one of their school commencements.

Perhaps the appearance of their present happy lot, and the knowledge of the hard, rough, cruel ways of the world before them, as yet untrod and unknown, is one reason. Perhaps also the certainty of the thought that many of them are going to be heart-broken in this life, and still others make everlasting shipwreck of character and the soul itself, adds to the peculiar burden.

Anyhow their bright, eager faces, fresh and pure lives, and innocent voices invariably bring to us a heart-melting and eye-filling experience.

* * * * *

The little fellows may not always be with us, but it pays anyhow to be patient with and kind to them. They have so much to learn. Everything is so new and strange to them, and oftentimes what is called a fault is simply ignorance.

Even if God spares them to us, and they grow up and go off in the wide, wide world to make their living, the memory of harsh words and a single cruel blow will be a perpetual ache to the heart. They will get enough of hard treatment without ours.

We read once of a father who, being much engrossed in his literary work, not only spoke roughly to his little boy pleading for something by his side, but dealt him a hasty blow with his hand.

The child perfectly heart-broken, withdrew at once. The father labored on at his desk, but could accomplish nothing. His ideas that had been flowing before, now utterly ceased. He could see but one picture between him and his manuscript, and that was first the pleading and then the grieved, sorrow-stricken face of his little boy. A great load bowed down his heart. He kept saying, "The child ought to know better than to annoy me when I am at my work." But the tearful face would not pass away.

After nearly an hour spent in the fruitless effort to write, he laid aside his pen and sought the child, whose mother had been dead for months. He was

not in the hall, nor on the porch, nor in the parlor.
Nor could he hear his voice anywhere. The whole
house was still.

Remembering an apartment that had been set
aside for him as a playroom, the father, walking
softly, found the little fellow asleep on the floor.

Before falling into slumber the child had gathered some of his simple playthings and, going into
a corner, tried to obtain comfort from them. With
his father angry, the rough word, the slap, and
order to go away, the world looked very dark to
the little one, and his only hope for consolation
was in his toys.

There they were around where he slept. He
had five or six shells in a row, and some pebbles he
had gathered in a walk, in another row. There
stood his little, squatty rubber doll with his round
comical face and two of his picture books. But
the funny looking doll could not win a smile from
his young owner today, and the shells and picture
books had lost their charm. The child had gone to
sleep grieving ; the eyelashes were heavy with un-
shed drops ; the face was stained with tears ; one had
dropped on the palm of his hand on which his cheek
rested, and each moment or so the little fellow
gave a kind of shivering sigh or sob in his sleep.

Tenderly gathering him in his arms, the father carried him to his study and laid him still asleep on a soft lounge near his desk. His own tears fell fast upon the child, whose patient sorrow and suffering completely melted him.

*　　*　　*　　*

Sometimes the little fellows trip away from us into heaven. It is surprising to see the number of small graves in the cemetery. Until death comes one can not realize how empty and desolate the translation of a child into the skies can make a large house.

We recall the experience of a gentleman who lost his only child, a little boy of eight years of age. In speaking of it, he said :

" Wife and I, when the evening comes on and the lamps are lighted, sit on opposite sides of the fireplace and think of him and talk about him with aching hearts. This is the hour he would come in from the yard or street where he had been at play. We know his little form is out in the cemetery, and yet we find ourselves listening still and waiting for him.

"Sometimes there has been a merry, boyish shout, so much like his voice, ringing from the street and echoing in the hall, that we have started up with beating hearts in the wild, sudden hope that he had come back. Then with a groan we would remember the little grave on the hillside and sink back in our chairs with a rush of blinding tears. Oh, that he could come back and put his little arms around our necks once more. Oh, to have him track up the hall with his muddy shoes, tease me for my knife, and beg me to fly his kite once more. Dear, dear boy, we did not dream, with all our love for him, that he had bound us with so many and such tender cords of affection and devotion.

"We wonder if he ever thinks of us in that beautiful land on high. Does he ever yearn to see us as we crave with breaking hearts to see him."

*   *   *   *

We recall a certain busy time in our life, when not only the tongue was in frequent demand before the public, but the pen had to fly for hours each day at home.

A certain little toddler in the family, aged about eighteen months, assumed that it was his privilege to break in at any time on these busy hours in the Study. He would escape from the notice of the family and his unsteady steps could instantly be recognized coming down the gallery to the room at the remote end, which had been fitted up as a kind of preacher's office or library. The room itself was a foot or more higher than the floor of the gallery.

The writer at his desk could hear the little uncertain footfalls approaching, could tell when he reached the door, and then, perfectly unable to write, would listen to the soft chubby fist striking several little blows at the bottom of the door. Not a word would be said on either side for several seconds, and then would come another soft beating of the tiny hand on the door.

It was no use, the pressing work had to be given up, the writing postponed. Somebody at the door, perfectly conscious of his power, was preparing to give the third series of knocks, when the door opened and he found himself lifted up and hugged tight in the arms of his father.

Somehow the postponed labor was performed afterwards, though at times it required a work deep in the night. But better than all, the father has been glad many times, since God took the little one to the skies, that the solemn-eyed, loving little fellow was never turned away a single time from the door. His gentle little knock was always honored.

XV.

A YOUNG MAN'S DEATH.

THERE is always something exceedingly pathetic to the writer in the spectacle of death. The tossing head, the heavy sighs, the restless movement of the limbs, and later, the gasping, lessening breath, are all unspeakably affecting. The last two or three respirations, that have a tremulous sound, remind us of the stifled sob of a tired, grieved child. Then when you had thought all was over, comes the last shivering sigh, the wearied breast sinks to rise no more, the chin droops, and then is seen the heart-sickening spectacle of it rising again and making a vain, last effort to bring air through the mouth into the exhausted lung. But there is not another breath. The chin falls again, and the eyes assume a fixed look as if gazing at things in eternity. The silver cord has been loosed, the golden bowl is broken, the pitcher broken at the fountain, and the mourners go about the streets. Another life is ended on earth forever.

Sad is the sight of death when viewed coming

upon the aged, but it is peculiarly affecting when witnessed in the young. The old must die, and many of them are glad to go. We expect them by the laws of nature to leave us. But for the young to lie down in the grave is a pathetic happening for a number of reasons.

When the writer was a pastor in a town in Mississippi, a physician requested him to call on a young traveling agent who was dying at a hotel in the place. He had arrived several days before a well man, was suddenly stricken down with disease, and had been informed by the doctor that day that he was a dying man. The wife had been telegraphed for, but the indications were that death would arrive before she did. Sadder still he was an unsaved man.

We found the sufferer in a single-roomed office that was located back of the hotel in a little vineyard. It had been fitted up as a bed-room, and was both cool and quiet.

The patient was something like thirty-five years of age. We found him with his head propped up on several pillows, and his eyes fixed in a steady gaze through the open window, at the leaves that were playing in the summer breeze on the sides of the vine-covered arbor. We doubt not that his eyes

went further than the shaded walk, and reached
his far away household, and back to his childhood
home, and all along the side of desecrated Sab-
baths, neglected churches, despised bibles, forgotton vows, and myriads of sins.

It must have been a heart-rending gaze, judging
by the melancholy face we saw when we entered;
and it was a sight that must have profoundly absorbed him, for he did not hear our step when
we entered. He must have been looking for Death
to come up the walk. Perhaps he was wondering
also whether he would see the form of his wife
approaching before Death arrived.

As he turned to behold us, when we spoke
something to him, he still had that anxious look in
his eyes, and bore one of the saddest expressions
we ever saw on living or dying face.

We were not allowed to remain long, but after
a brief and faithful conversation, asked him to
allow us to pray for him. He consented, and we
were so drawn out in his behalf that we not only
agonized in supplication for him, but did so for quite
a while. The tears dripped from our face as we
plead for an immortal soul, which we felt was so
close to eternity.

On arising from our knees we begged him to

pardon us for having prayed so long. His affecting reply as he fixed his sorrowful black eyes upon us was, "No one can pray too long for me now."

As we left the room we saw his head turn again to its former position, and the eyes resume the old melancholy watch down the shaded arbor walk, where the vine leaves fluttered and glanced in the morning sunlight.

In a few hours two forms came up the walk ; one was Death, and the other the wife. They arrived in the order just mentioned.

We saw the bereaved woman with bowed head, in a carriage next day, following a hearse that had in it the dead body of her husband. She was on the way to the depot, and beginning a lonely journey of hundreds of miles back to her fatherless children and desolated home. Many eyes were wet on that day when people on the street glanced from the hearse, and took note of the black-robed young woman who sat bowed and solitary in the carriage.

*   *   *   *

Another instance comes to the writer of a character somewhat different.

A mother and son living in one of our large cities had been everything to each other. We scarcely ever witnessed greater devotion. He toiled hard as a mail carrier to support the family. Finally he fell sick, and we doubt not it was entirely from overwork. It proved to be a fatal stroke.

In the long illness which preceded his death, the mother scarcely ever left the side of his bed. One day he looked at her and said ·

"I feel so very sorry for you, mother."

With a choking voice she answered :

"Why, my son?"

"Because we have been everything to each other, and when I am gone you will be so lonely, and will miss me."

Her heart was too full to reply.

At last the day of death came. Struggling for breath he gazed at her and said :

" Mother, is this death?"

Taking his hand in hers, and choking back her grief, she said :

" Yes, my son, this is death."

He lay back on the pillow pale and gasping, and then with a smile playing upon his lips, said :

" I am ready."

As he lay thus with his eyes closed, and with the same distressing gasp for breath, the mother bent over him and said :

"Oh, my son, have you not a comforting word for your mother?"

Opening his eyes with a tender and affectionate light in them, he said:

"I love you, mother."

The eyes closed again. The breast heaved under a great suffocating pressure, while the mother bending over him heard him whisper:

"Almost home!"

A few moments afterward he looked up and his lips moved the last time. Anxious to hear the faintest syllable, the mother bent closely and caught the word:

"Rest!"

The breath left the body, but the eyes remained fixed on the mother with the same old loving, devoted look. The soul had ascended, but Elijah-like, had flung back, as it left, its own beautiful affection in the face and eyes.

In a minute more the lids drooped, and the mother laying her hands upon them closed them upon the world forever.

XVI.

ON one of my trips I landed in a large city of several thousand inhabitants. Having occasion to visit a dentist I secured the name and number of a good one, and in due time found myself on the fifth floor of a monster modern building and wandering down the marble-floored hall to the office designated.

A young girl of seventeen, whom I caught flirting with a young man of spidery extremities and a gosling voice, told me that Dr. Klem was absent but would be back in a few minutes.

The waiting-room and office were both very handsomely and tastefully furnished. Two oil paintings and several pastels hung on the walls, while easy chairs, a richly carved table loaded with magazines, and a large upright music box were present to contribute their diversion and consolation to the visitors who came to pay their painful visits.

The Doctor soon arrived and at once impressed me as a man of considerable mental force and thoroughly well bred.　He had a pale, intellectual face, with dark eyes, and dark beard trimmed close, after the Vandyke style.　His dress was a business suit of dark gray, while three large links of a gold chain appeared at his vest.　His manner at once put me at ease, and in a minute impressed me with perfect confidence in his professional ability.

As he proceeded in his work, my eye took in the lines of strength about his face and mouth, the conviction deepening all the while that he was a man who had been endowed with great self-control, or had learned it in some school of sorrow.　I also detected signs of physical weariness, and ventured to ask him if he was not an overworked man.

His reply was, that frequently he was ten and twelve hours a day on his feet, that his business had greatly increased, so that often he had missed his mid-day meal, and frequently did night work to fulfill his engagements ; that all this, he supposed, with the bent attitude of the body in his dental task, was doubtless telling on him.

Just then the office girl announced the presence of his wife, and the inner door opened, causing the music box to play, by some electric connection, one of the popular street ballads.

The lady who entered was good looking, but had lost a certain freshness hard to describe. She was thirty years of age, but looked older. Her clothes were of the best material, but they lacked a harmonizing of colors, while several inches of a white skirt protruded on one side. A large lock of her blonde hair was straggling down the back of her neck, and her tan shoes needed a polishing.

The woman had a deep wrinkle on her brow, a nervous motion of the hands, and a querulous, almost whining tone of voice. The Doctor gravely glanced up as she entered, and as quickly let his eyes fall on his work the next second.

" Where was Jennie when I came here an hour ago? " she almost demanded.

" She went to her luncheon," replied the husband, as he drilled with great care a small cavity in a frail tooth.

We could hear the wife fidgeting around in the outer room. " Office so dirty," came the sentence like a steel arrow through the glass partition.

" Yes, the wind blew some dust up from the street through the windows, but not much." This was said with effort, for he had delicate work on hand needing all his attention. I wondered that the woman could not see it.

"You may think it all right, but I think the room is simply dreadful," was the minnie-ball answer.

After this we could hear her fidgeting about the outer apartments.

"Whose porcelain box is this?"

"Mine."

"Where did you get it"

"A gentleman friend gave it to me,"

"I'll take it home for the parlor. You don't want it."

"All right," was the calm reply.

Then followed the sound of drawers being pulled open, doors of desks shut, etc., etc.

She had just come from a nobby restaurant and was fresh and exhilarated from a cup of tea that had been flanked by a chicken sandwich and a large slice of strawberry cake. The dentist had been so busy that day that he had not found time to get his lunch. It was now nearly four o'clock and the man had a tired, faint look in his face, though the square chin, steady eyes, and firm mouth showed that the spirit was unconquered and was still in the line of habitual self-control.

It took but a few glances from the patient in the chair to see that the domestic magpie, hopping around in her faded beauty and trailing underskirt, was a greater trial and suffering to the man than the ten hours long work without rest or food.

He had just bought a house for her that day, and the half hour which he usually gave to his luncheon he had spent in a lawyer's office arranging deeds that conveyed the property as his gift to her in fee simple. This explained his absence from the office on our first arrival.

The woman of course was glad about the property, but at the same time took it very much as a matter of course. And here, at a time when from the nature of the work he was doing the man needed to be perfectly unmolested, she was firing volleys of questions at him as to when they would move, and who would move them, what it would cost, etc., etc., etc,

Then came the old querulous, whining tone again.

"I don't know where I'll put the base burner."

"We'll find a place."

Some more fidgeting and then,

"It's a pretty house, but oh the trouble in moving. I'm sure I'll be sick and in bed after it's all over."

No sound but the faint drill of one of the dentist's instruments.

Then the female drill began again,

"I wonder who is going to move us? If that man Johnson does it again, we won't have a sound piece of furniture left in the house."

"I've secured Higgins to do it," said the quiet voice of the Doctor over me. Glancing up I thought the lines of the face were much deeper than when I first saw them.

"Well, I suppose I must go," said the Nerve Drill in skirts. "I believe I will run around and take a peep at the house before I go home. And, oh, don't forget to stop at the grocer's and order a sugar-cured ham; I want some for supper. And where do you reckon Jimmie has gone? he didn't come home from school to-day.

The Dentist replied to all his wife said, kindly, but with a wearied accent that was unspeakably pathetic. The patient marvelled how he could perform the work he was doing and stand the hoppings of that domestic magpie around the two offices and answer the querulous notes she dropped, as she skipped and skimmed about.

By and by she left.

Later on the office girl announced a lady in the

ante-room. The doctor disappeared, and in a few minutes reappeared with the request that I would vacate the chair a few minutes while he gave relief to a young lady who was suffering from the pressure of a small gold plug.

The young lady came in, a handsome, stylish looking girl, and evidently from the best social circles. Her tailor-made gown fitted to perfection, the plume on her hat drooped becomingly over her dark eyes. She held an American Beauty in her hand, which she gave to the Doctor. He placed the rose in a glass of water on a cabinet shelf near him, and a pleased smile came over his somewhat melancholy face for a moment.

A very excellent thing is a soft, low voice in a woman. And the girl in the chair had it. Even when the doctor with dexterous fingers and instruments was relieving the pressure of the gold filling in the sensitive tooth, and would put short queries, her equally terse replies, in spite of finger gags and other mufflers of speech, would be little murmuring sounds full of liquid music.

As she rested upon the crimson cushions of the operating chair, the lines of her fine figure were full of grace and beauty. The aroma of the rose filled the room, but the perfume of the flower had a greater rival in a sweeter fragrance still, and that was the subtile, softening, refining atmosphere or influence of a womanly woman.

A canary bird commenced singing in its cage, a south wind blew gently in through the open window, and a hand-organ, from a distant street corner, could just be heard playing, "The Sweetest Story ever Told."

*   *   *   *

Two months after this, in another brief visit to the city, I happened to be passing the office and started to enter, intending to express my satisfaction with the dental work done before and to inform Dr. Klem that on my next trip to the city I would call upon him to make some additional touches. But as I paused at the door I saw the Doctor was engaged, and turned away. In that moment's pause, however, I was struck with a change I observed in him. The side of his face was turned toward me, but its pallor was plainly noticeable from the door, while the lines about the still strong face were graver and deeper than when I last saw him. I noticed also that a fresh American Beauty was blooming where we had seen him place the first flower.

*   *   *   *

Several months subsequent to the scene just
mentioned, I ascended the elevator of the Big Sky
Scraper and, reaching the Doctor's floor, walked
down the corridor toward his office. To my great
surprise the door was shut and locked as well.
From the transom overhead I could see there was
no light in the office, but all was somber and
still. There was no answer to repeated raps, and
I could not get my consent to peep through the
key hole.

Just then the gosling young man I had seen on my
first visit was hurriedly passing. So I said quickly,

"Where is Doctor Klem?"

"Why," he said, hastening on, but turning
upon me a look of surprise, "Haven't you heard
about the Doctor?"

"No—what is it?"

"John!" cried a loud voice up the corridor,
and the gosling vanished in a distant office.

As I stood wondering in the hall, two ladies
drew near, and as they passed Dr. Klem's door,
they glanced at the sign and one said,

"Isn't is sad about Dr. Klem?"

"Dreadful," replied the other.

"They say," continued the first, "that Mrs.
Klem is perfectly crushed.

"Yes. Poor thing, I don't wonder."

The ladies swept on, and I followed them, debating in my mind the propriety of stopping and asking them to relieve my anxiety about the Doctor, but before I could decide they turned into an office partly filled with ladies and gentlemen, and the door closed upon them. Before I lost sight of them they had dropped two other words, but for my life I could not certainly tell what they were.

One was "brokenhearted" or "departed." The other was "dead" or "fled."

I made one more effort before leaving the building to discover the truth. As I got to the foot of the elevator, and people were rushing out of it, others hastening in, the signal bell ringing from every one of the fifteen floors above us, and the elevator youth looking worn and worried, I made bold to ask him, just as he was about to take his upward flight with a crowded car,

"Did you know Dr. Klem?"

"Yes, of course I did."

"Well, what's the matter with him, and what has become of him?"

The youth gave me a strange indescribable look, touched his lever and shot out of sight with his passengers, without having opened his lips.

XVII.

WE do not fail to recognize in the matter of personal religious experience many shades of difference, proceeding from temperament, education and other causes. Nevertheless the foundational work is compelled to be the same, and the testimony of the Spirit to one's relation to God is a universal privilege. Many individuals, therefore, with but little outward demonstration are as soundly regenerated and sanctified as those whose noisy overflow commands the attention of gazing hundreds.

While this is true, we must confess, however, to a wonderful partiality for those cases which give no feeble or uncertain note when the fire of heaven falls upon them. Out of a number that memory recalls we give two or three instances.

In one of our Western states lived an unconverted man, who owned a store and was doing a prosperous business. Among other things which he sold was whiskey by the bottle, jug or barrel. He was thriving so well that he gave his store a

new coat of paint and treated it to a brand new
sign, which swung and creaked in front.

One day a farmer, who was a friend and acquaintance, came into the store and asked him to
let him have a drink of liquor, that he was
tired and cold. The merchant in reply gave him
a key to one of the barrels and told him to help
himself. A half hour or so rolled by, and the merchant had forgotton all about the circumstance,
when a gentleman strolled into the store, leaned
on the counter and said to him slowly and
solemnly, .

"I see your sign is lying flat in the road."

"What !" exclaimed the storekeeper, and rushed
out on the gallery expecting to behold his new sign
down on the ground. To his great relief there it
swung in its place near the ceiling.

"No," he said, turning to his informer, "my
sign is not down ; what made you say so?"

"Yes it is," persisted the gentleman. "It is
further down the road."

The storekeeper followed the pointing finger
and beheld, forty yards down the street, in the
middle of the highway, the prostrate form of the
man to whom he had given the key of the whiskey
barrel. He was dead drunk.

The sight was like an arrow to the heart of the beholder, and crying out, "My God, is that the sign of my store!" he walked into his store and closed the door behind him.

He never sold another drop of liquor from that hour.

Then followed days of unspeakable anguish of mind and heart through the convicting power of the Holy Ghost. He could not eat, sleep, rest or attend to business.

There grew around the town, and extending deep into the country, dense thickets. Taking his axe he penetrated the jungle and cut out a place in which to pray. He spent an hour in his leafy cavern, and failing to find relief, he went out and, a hundred yards away, hewed a second nook for prayer. Still finding no deliverance, he prepared a third. But as he prayed in it his burden seemed to increase. He then returned to the first, next visited the second and wound up in the third, praying in great and growing agony in them all.

Thus he did for several days, until one morning while in one of his caves calling on God for mercy, the blessing of salvation was poured into his heart and he shouted for joy.

His hallelujahs were heard a quarter of a mile

away at a United States military post, and officers
and men both thinking that it was an outbreak of the
Indians, a corporal and squad of soldiers were sent
running toward the town.   Guided by the whoops
and yells, they dashed into the thicket where our
new convert was having the whole war to
himself.

Filled with a rapturous love, he flung himself
on the corporal and hugged him, and attempted to
embrace all the soldiers, when the corporal, at first
stupefied and now still mystified, but also deeply
disgusted, cried out to his men :

"About face !   Double quick ! " and went back
in a swinging trot to the garrison.

After this our brother joined the church and
for months greatly enjoyed his new found salvation.

One of the idols of the past life, however,
which he would not give up, was his pipe.   He
felt disturbed about it at times, and had occasional
gloomy spells, but still was moving along.

Soon after this there came to his western village
a Holiness evangelist, when he found that under
his searching sermons his moodiness was increasing.   But still he puffed away at his tobacco and
did considerable grumbling.

One morning the preacher, who was watching

him load his pipe preparatory to putting a coal of fire on it, said:

"My brother, would you be willing to swap that filthy old pipe for a clean heart and a sweet family altar?"

At once he became very angry in spirit and with difficulty kept from being rude to the minister. He felt that he was being very hardly dealt with, that his rights were ignored, his privileges trampled upon, and he was being tormented before the time. In a word, he fumed. He remained in this state several hours, getting what consolation he could from his pipe; and he never obtained less.

Toward the middle of the day he was a mile from town in his two-horse wagon, filling it with large stones for one of his fences. The pipe lay unsmoked in his pocket, and the rocks seemed to get in his breast. Grimly and with groans he worked until the vehicle was nearly loaded.

He stopped a moment to rest as he stood on the boulders. A sweet inner voice whispered, "Surely you would not keep out the Comforter because of an unclean habit."

At once there sprang into his mind and heart the determination, "I will give up everything for God!" Running his hands in his pockets he pulled out his pipe and tobacco pouch and threw them as far as he could into the forest. They had scarcely left his hands when the baptism of the Holy Ghost and fire fell upon him.

With cries of joy and tears of rapture rolling down his cheeks, he gathered the reins in his hands, turned the galloping horses homeward, and came flying down the road, filling the air with his shouts and the highway with all the stones he had gathered.

The town, attracted by the outcries and rattle of the wagon, turned out to meet him as he swept into the square. They thought he had lost his mind, but he told them from his wheeled pulpit that it was his carnal mind that was gone. Oh, how he preached! His wagon indeed was empty, but he himself was full. He had given up the last of his old idols, and got in exchange a clean heart and a sweet family altar—in a word, the blessing of full salvation.

The writer saw him two years after the transaction had taken place, and he was still pre-eminently satisfied.

*   *   *   *

In some of our meetings we have beheld scenes, and witnessed works of the Spirit, which, if put in print, would read like occurrences in the days of Wesley and of the Apostles.

In a certain town in a Western State the services were held in the Opera House. We had a number of clear conversions and powerful sanctifications. Among the latter was one that was quite remarkable.

For days the man had been patiently and persistently seeking the blessing. Just as I had concluded a morning sermon, and while a number were approaching the altar, the Holy Fire fell upon him. The scene which followed was simply beyond any proper description. The power upon him, and in him was so great that the man looked like one electrified, and to the world would have appeared to have been in an agony. He was literally flung about the house by an invisible but uncontrollable force. He would sink down a moment on his knees in a rapture of joy, only the next moment to be lifted suddenly to his feet and swept away to a distant part of the building. I thought several times that chairs would be broken and the stage scenery before which we were preaching would all be demolished under one of his amazing rushes! But nothing of the kind took place. All could see who watched the man that not a

particle of "put on" or "worked up" was in
the case.   God was simply pleased to make an
individual a spectacle of His power, and show that
a live gospel was still in the world, and that the
Holy Ghost had not exhausted Himself on the
day of Pentecost.

It was fully a half hour before the man had
calmed down in a measure. A crowd of men rushed
up from the street, and with faces as solemn as death
viewed the scene of a hundred holiness people in
a spiritual rapture, salvation flowing at the altar,
and a man whom they knew, filled with the Holy
Ghost and fairly caught away from the world in
which he lived.

As I studied the case before me, I could not but
think of the description of the man in the Book of
Acts who was saved by the power of Jesus' name,
and went "leaping and praising God through the
Temple." This man was not in the Temple, but he
did not leap or praise God the less, because he had
found full salvation in an opera house. Perhaps
Christ had in his mind these days of ecclesiastical ex-
iledom of full salvation, when He said :   " Woman
believe me, the hour cometh, when ye shall neither
in this mountain, nor yet at Jerusalem, worship the
Father.   But the hour cometh and now is when the

true worshipers shall worship the Father in spirit
and in truth.''

It is blessed, indeed, to find that God is not confined to times and places. He is everywhere. And
to the soul perfectly redeemed, every house is a
temple, the mists of the morning is incense, the
birds are a part of the heavenly choir, while every
bush and shrub by the roadside, burns and sparkles
with the glory of God.

*　　*　　*　　*

On the third, fourth and fifth days of a meeting God began to stretch certain individuals out
on the floor around the altar in the old-fashioned
way. I was deeply interested in the case of a
Methodist local preacher of fully sixty years of
age, who sought the blessing of sanctification with
a persistence and patience for five days that I never
saw surpassed. Morning and night he was the
first at the altar, and sought the blessing with
strong crying and tears. Service after service he
failed to obtain the witness of the Spirit that the
work was done, yet he never allowed himself to be
discouraged. Others swept in ahead of him who
had begun later, but he did not murmer, repine,
halt, nor fall into darkness, on account of what to
some would have appeared divine favoritism. He

held on in his lonely way. He told the Lord that he must have the blessing. He did not kneel a little while and then get up and take his seat, as I have seen many do, but he held on to the horns of the altar, and pleaded with God, while great tears rolled down his cheeks and fell upon the rail before him. Meantime his soul was greatly blessed in the seeking. He was evidently in the path of the just that shineth more and more unto the perfect day. He was nearing Canaan, and stood on the banks of Jordan in the same beautiful country that so captivated two of the tribes of Israel that they would not cross over at all. Alas for people who stop short of entire sanctification with any religious experience, no matter how good it is. The word is, "Cross over."

Mr. Wesley says that sanctification is preceded and followed by a blessed growth in grace. All sanctified people find it so. It pays spiritually just to seek sanctification. The soul wakes up, the spirit gets on a stretch for better things, the heart becomes inflamed with love and devotion to God. But it pays better to "go on to perfection," to "groan after it," and never stop until we are "made perfect in love in this life." See the Discipline, and above all see the Bible.

Our local preacher spent a couple of blessed days on the beautiful banks of Jordan, but still sighing out his soul for Canaan beyond the flood. One night nearly everyone had left the altar but himself; he still lingered with great pleadings before God, when suddenly the Savior whispered to him, " He that confesseth me before men, him will I confess before my Father which is in heaven." He leaped to his feet, crying, " I believe He sanctifies me now "—when instantly the power of God came upon him, the fire fell, and there followed a scene that the congregation of that night will never forget. Oh how he shouted, laughed, wept, clapped his hands, and embraced his brethren. Did any of my readers ever hear a man rejoice who had not thus overflowed in twenty, thirty or forty years, who was doing the first real shouting of his life? As a rule such people make up for lost time. Besides, the Holy Ghost can make a first-class shouter in a single second. There is needed no evolution or growth into this Methodistic, old-time religion, pentecostal and heavenly overflow of the heart and exercise of the voice. So our brother shouted, and cried out he was sanctified, and shouted some more, and said he had the witness—that the Spirit told him he had the blessing. Then he shouted again, and went over to his weeping wife at the altar, and said to her, " Say, glory," and then fell back on the floor and clapped his hands over his head and shouted again.

Other men were quietly saved that night, but his case drew special attention and interest because of his being a preacher, and his having sought the blessing so long and patiently. What some one has called "The Problem of Methodism" was solved with him forever; and so it would be with all who would do as he did. If our preachers and laymen who fight the doctrine of instantaneous sanctification by faith, would spend the time and energy in seeking for the blessing which they now lose in withstanding it, there would soon be no "Problem of Methodism" to discuss, while the glorious solution, read in shining faces, liberated tongues, and God-empowered lives, would send a revival wave of salvation over this land whose tidal uplift would bear upon it the beautiful dawn of the Millennium.

XVIII.

A PRODIGY is a marvel. Looking at it in a geographical sense, it is something or somebody not far removed from the boundary line of the miraculous. The word naturally leads to other words like prodigious ; while some say that the prodigy of the household often turns into a prodigal. We do not stop to argue this question.

Prodigies are known to exist in different forms as well as in different fields of life and nature. Usually, however, they are quite scarce everywhere except in the home circle.

If anyone would see a prodigy without any loss of time, let him knock at the first house where dwells a mother with a group of children, and she will point out one or several without a moment's hesitation.

It is exceedingly gratifying to a lover of the race, and especially a patriot, to be made to realize the amount of genius, the quantity of undeveloped greatness that is in the children of every family. If he is doubtful, the mother can soon convince him he is wrong and give him overwhelming proofs of the marvelous gifts and talents she has recognized in her boys.

The father, having been a boy, is more conservative in his opinions of "that wonderful child" or "that remarkable boy." Some would call him distrustful and others downright skeptical. Still others declare that he is really hard hearted to smile so grimly when his wife is enlarging upon the transcendent abilities of George Frederick Adolphus.

His lack of cordial agreement, and even silence, fails however to move the mother, who continues to write to distant members of the family connection about the amazing sayings and wonderful doings of a certain little fellow in knee pants. She "fears she will never be able to raise him." She "is confident that death has marked him for its own." She "just knows that no child with such wise and profound speeches, so far beyond his years, will ever live." She "listens to him with a sinking heart." She "writes these lines with overflowing eyes as she is convinced that William Henry Robinson will never be spared in this sinful world." "But if he does live, she knows that he will be President of the United States or Bishop of the Episcopal Church," etc., etc., etc.

It is said that all Jewish mothers hoped to bring forth the Messiah into the world. To-day women dream of being the mother of generals, admirals, orators, bishops and presidents.

Who can count the G. W.'s, H. C.'s, D. W.'s, A. J.'s, M. L.'s, J. W.'s, and N. B.'s of this world. Interpreted, these letters stand for George Washington, Henry Clay, Daniel Webster, Andrew Jackson, Martin Luther, John Wesley, and Napoleon Bonaparte. We have found several of the latter among the colored people.

Every mother with a boy child seems to think she has brought a prodigy into the world, and if he is not already one, well, he will be one.

Two things amaze the author in this connection. One is the number of ordinary children in all the homes in the land, and the other is the vast number of ordinary people everywhere. What becomes of these wonders of the household? Did their genius evaporate after they were ten years of age? Did envy plot to keep them down and hide their light? Or (perish the thought) were the mothers mistaken about their greatness?

One thing is certain, that instead of the nation being filled with blazing geniuses, we find vast bodies of plain, plodding men bearing the initials of G. W., D. W., J. W., A. J., H. C., and N. B. ; the nearest approach they ever make to greatness and celebrity.

The family and kindred of the writer had as many prodigies as any other household, considering all things. Among them was a boy relative of the author, who, construing his mother's dreams of his abilities to be facts, announced to us that he intended to be Emperor of the United States, and when he got seated on the throne, he would give us the State of Mississippi as a Princedom. We dreamed of this elevation for many months. Our title was to be Prince of Mississippi ; his, the Emperor of the United States. We think he intended taking in Mexico and Canada later on, when he got finally seated.

In a family residing near us, there were not less than four prodigies. Three of them would not believe it, and so refusing to ascend the pedestal, remained ordinary boys and are to-day ordinary men.

But the fourth graciously received the maternal prophecies and prognostications, and added to the sum of the original statement a compound interest of personal expectation and general day dreaming of his own. One day while wandering through the

fields near his home, he entered a deep cut made
for the passage of the country road, through a
ridge, and observing the smooth surface of the red
clay walls on either hand, he could not refrain from
carving with his barlow knife in very large letters
and in a very conspicuous place on the bank, his
own name in full, and underneath that, quite a startling piece of information. The words were:

"CHARLES AUGUSTUS SMITH,
The Hope of The South."

Having thus relieved himself, Charles Augustus
climbed up on the top of the bank and lay down to
hear unseen the comment of the passersby. It was
not long before he heard one. He wished afterward that he had not listened.

An old farmer was jogging along on his way
to a grist mill with a sack of corn on his horse.
He happened to observe the huge lettering on the
smooth red clay. Stopping his horse and putting
on his spectacles, he read with great deliberation;

" Charles Agustus Smith,
The Hope of the South."

The two sentences seemed to interest him very
much, for he read them over three times, and rubbed his chin and scratched his jaw vigorously
while he did so. Finally, taking off his glasses and

putting them back in their tin case with a snap, he started off down the road in a jog trot, and looking back over his shoulder, as his elbows flapped against his sides, he said aloud, not dreaming he was heard :

" Well, if that's so—we are gone ! "

Perhaps it might be well to state that the South for some reason utterly failed to look to and lean upon Charles Augustus in her troubles, and so came to her final defeat and ruin. The public may now know for the first time why the seceding States failed.

It might also be well to add that Mr. Smith, whose prefix is Charles Augustus, has been patiently following a mule up and down various corn and cotton furrows ever since the " Surrender," engaged in the absorbing task of providing certain necessaries of life, like bread and meat, for a Mrs. Amanda Malvina Smith, and seven little Smiths, all of whom, no doubt, are prodigies, just as was their father before them.

XIX.

THE first time we ever met Walter Puzzled, he was twenty years of age. He had been soundly converted and was deeply spiritual, with an exceedingly tender conscience gravitating toward the morbid line.

Raised in a denomination which believed in immersion, he had become captivated with the spirit and polity of the Methodist church. Called to preach the gospel, and in harmony with most of the doctrines of Methodism, he was deeply desirous of laboring in her borders and with her people, but was kept back from the step by the simple fact that he did not believe in Infant Baptism.

He had given up his belief in immersion, with other doctrines of the denomination to which he belonged; was deeply attached to the Methodist people, and a warm defender of her tenets, but there was the Infant Baptism question, which he could not agree to, and not believing in that, his conscientious mind would not allow him to take the step of joining the followers of Wesley and making application to preach in their midst.

There was the call to preach burning in his soul ; there were the Methodists ready to receive him and license him to preach ; there was the wide world lying all around with souls perishing for the gospel ; but there also was that Infant Baptism problem which he could not solve, and which he felt must be settled before he could enter the fields which he himself admitted were white unto the harvest.

Bro. Puzzled lived on the farm of his parents, about two miles from the town where the writer of this sketch was stationed. So that he saw him frequently, both at his home, on the street, and in church on the Sabbath. But whenever he beheld him he always bore on his face the anxious, intent look of a man working out a tremendous problem. The far-away look in his eye, the dreamy voice, the corrugated brow almost gave one the headache in pure sympathy for the mental labor going on.

It mattered not where we came across Brother Puzzled, he carried with him that anxious and abstracted look. Sitting with the family on the front porch, or gazing at the preacher from his pew, or leaning against his father's barn, or resting cross-legged on the fence, he always carried that mystified look with him. He was wrestling with the Infant Baptism question.

He told the writer at different times, with months between, that he thought he was obtaining light on the subject: but his face did not indicate it, and his actions, or rather non-action, gainsaid the speech.

After twelve months' acquaintance with young Puzzled, the Conference to which the writer belonged sent him to a distant work, where in a year's time he secured two churches for his denomination, one deeded, the other built; had a number of revivals, saw several hundred people converted and join the church, and then returned on a visit to the town where Brother Puzzled lived, to find that he was mentally and problematically just where he had left him a year before.

He never felt, he said, the call to preach clearer. He never felt the need to go out at once and save perishing souls more so than now, but he could not yet see his way clear to go on account of the Infant Baptism question. Still he thought he was getting light, and he had told his father and mother that they must prepare to give him up, and run the farm with his brother, who was a year younger than himself.

Our next absence was one of two years in length. In the meantime, being in another part of the State, we heard nothing of our friend. So on arrival we at once asked if he had Joined the church or gone into the ministry, and was answered in the negative by a gentleman who was interested in him. He said that Brother Puzzled was troubled about the Infant Baptism question.

We learned from another party who had known Walter Puzzled longer than the other, that the question was getting deeper with him, that George, the younger brother, told him that Walter studied the subject so deeply and so absorbingly that he would lean motionless on his plow or sit buried in thought on the fence, while he (George) would run four or five furrows.

"Sometimes," said George, "I feel like protesting to brother Walter, and telling him to do his plowing in the day and think over that Infant Baptism question at night; that his worrying over that doctrine is putting double work on me; but he looks so much in earnest about the matter that I have not the heart to tell him that I am doing my work on the farm and his also."

This spirit of protest was only occasional with George. As a rule he felt proud of Walter, not that he had accomplished anything in life, but was going to do so. He felt that his brother was marked for a high calling and great destiny; that while he was a little slow in getting at his work, yet this he was sure was occasioned by the magnitude of the doctrinal problem and the tremendous nature of the conclusions that Walter was about to draw from his reflections. So that the deeper Walter's cogitations were, the more profoundly impressed was George.

One day when Walter Puzzled was thirty years old, still talking about the life-calling awaiting him, and the work he was yet to do, his father said :

"My son, I believe you think your life-work is going to come up the road to meet you headed by a brass band."

The son looked so pained at this that the father alluded to the matter no more.

When he was thirty-five years old, with the problem still unsolved, a blunt-spoken preacher gave him a great shock by saying :

"And so, Walter, a question of a few spoon-fuls of water on a baby's head has kept you out of the active service of God for fifteen years."

Walter coughed and cleared his throat and said his conscience would not let him be a Methodist preacher, when he did not believe in Infant Baptism.

"Well, then, be a Baptist preacher," urged his friend.

"I can not," he replied, "because I do not believe in the doctrines of that church."

"Well, what are you going to do? Will you sit on the fence all the days of your life, getting ready to make a start, to begin to commence to do something?"

Walter swallowed a big lump in his throat and answered,

"As soon as I settle the Infant Baptism question, I expect to enter the active work of the ministry."

"The preacher looked at him steadily for a moment and said,

"If the mothers of the land put a gallon of water on their children every day in the name of decency and cleanliness, I do not think that God will count it a sin on your part if you pour a cupful on their heads in the name of the Lord, who made both the water and the child!"

The last time we saw Walter Puzzled he was forty years old, and his hair gray. He was still on the farm and, so to speak, still on the fence. He still sat on stumps and logs in deep meditation, and still cogitated in the field, resting on the beam of his plow, while George, now a married man, would throw up five furrows to his one. Myriads of sinners had died and gone to hell, whom God had called him to warn and save, but the qnestion of the application of a cupful of water to an innocent baby had been such a grave matter to him that he could not leave it to attend to a life call, and a divine call at that, of everlasting moment.

All the new preachers who came to the town as pastors would be much taken with Walter at first. They would have long talks with him, loan him books on baptism, etc., etc. But after a few months they would begin to wear peculiar smiles when his name was mentioned, give a dry cough and even laugh aloud.

Five years have passed since we last saw Walter. He is now a white haired man of forty-five. Recently the writer met a preacher, who had just been sent to the town near which Brother Puzzled resides. He told us that there was a very interesting case two miles from town.

We of course begged for information.

He then informed us that there was a deeply spiritual man who came to his church, and was

undoubtedly called of God to preach, and could he
be once convinced, would do great good in the
the world, but he would not join his church, or
enter the ministry because of a single doctrinal
difficulty.

"May I tell you what it is?" we asked.

"Yes, if you can."

"It is the question of Infant Baptism," we
replied.

"How did you know that," asked the preacher.

"Because he has been worrying with it a
quarter of a century.   In 1875 he was right where
you see him to-day."

The preacher gave a long, low whistle.

If you see him again soon, tell him, please, that
you heard a man say that twenty-five years ago he
was the most spiritual and promising every way of
a dozen young Christian men whom he knew in
his town ; that eleven of these young men have
gone forth under the leadings of Christ and brought
thousands of souls to God, while he, naturally
more gifted, and once far ahead of them spiritually,
has lost a lifetime in worrying over a non-essential
doctrine.

XX.

THE DISCONTENTED MAN.

SOME time since, while on a southern trip, we encountered a character at the table of a hotel. He possessed a querulous voice, fault-finding nature, and was of course a discontented man. He wore the wearied look belonging to such a spirit. As we studied his case, he seemed to be continually apprehensive that various and sundry personal rights would be taken from or denied him.

One morning at breakfast he called for "aigs," as he called them. As the waiter started to leave, he cried out after him,

"I don't want them aigs hard boiled."

Then followed several minutes of anxious waiting upon his part. He kept turning his head restlessly toward the door which led to the kitchen. Finally, at the expiration of four or five minutes, he fairly wailed out to the invisible servant,

"I just know them aigs is hard boiled."

It would be impossible to transcribe in words the look of trouble on the man's face, and the accent of sorrow, not to say despair, in his voice, as he prophesied and grieved about the eggs.

The air, look and voice perfectly agreed in protestation and lamentation. It was evident to anyone at a glance that at this moment, to this man, the world was a mockery and life itself a failure, and all because "them aigs were hard boiled."

As we continued to study the bereaved individual before us, we realized again not only the blessedness, but the philosophy of full salvation; that God had a work of grace for the soul, which enables one to rejoice, not only when certain things are not to one's notion, but even in the loss of all things to be self-contained and happy. The perfectly tranquil life is that, where the man says Amen at the severing of every cord which binds him to earth and earthly things. It is these very terrestrial objects which create such disturbance in the human heart and life, and so that grace of God, which breaks their charm and sweeps away their power, will of necessity bring a reign of unbroken peace and holy gladness to the soul.

Some months after this occurrence we were spending a few days in a large boarding house in a city several hundred miles from the town just mentioned. One morning, while glancing over a newspaper, in the large reading room allotted to the guests, there came in through the open window from the gallery outside a perfect string of vocal jerking sounds like Bah! Pooh! Pshaw! Bosh! Nonsense! Botheration! These were accompanied by an angry rustling of a newspaper, scraping of the chair, and now and then the fall of a heavy heel on the floor.

The voice with its nasal, whining intonation was masculine and strangely familiar. Rising up and going to the window, we saw, tilted back on two legs of a chair, with his feet high up against a post, our friend who had wailed so over the "hard boiled aigs."

The lady of the house happened at the time to be passing through the rooms, and we asked her if she knew anything about the gentleman who was reading the paper out on the porch.

At once she began smiling, and taking a seat remote from the window she, with difficulty, straightened her face, and said :

" That's Mr. Spears. Everybody around here knows him. He is a man of some little property and travels around a good deal. He is too restless to stay anywhere long. He seems to be

soured with the whole world and nothing pleases
him."

"Is he a sick man?" we asked.

"No, indeed. There's nothing the matter with
him that way, though he insisted for a long time
there was. He went to all the Springs in the
country, and every health resort in the mountains
or on the sea shore. He has had every physician
in his town at one time or another, and discharged
them all, saying they didn't have sense enough to
know what was the matter with him. He said it
was the doctor's business to find out the trouble
and cure a man, and that they could if they were doctors ; but they are all quacks these days, he says."

Very much interested, I kept silent, while the
lady went on.

"The last physician discharged Mr. Spears and
told him there was nothing in the world the matter
with him, but to follow a pair of plow handles to
make his own bread, instead of having it come in
to him without a struggle. He told him that any
man who ate as much as he did ought never to go
to the Springs for an appetite, or say he was sick.
Mr. Spears fairly foamed at this speech, but he had
to take it, for the doctor was a big man and fully
able to stand by what he said."

" What is the matter with Mr. Spears this morning?" I inquired. "He seems to be all out of sorts."

"Oh, he's just reading the newspaper. He allows what he sees there to completely upset him. He believes all that the reporters and editors and correspondents say, and is thrown into a regular fever every time he takes up the paper. He is firmly convinced that everything is going to the dogs ; declares there have been no great men since the days of Daniel Webster and Henry Clay, no president since Andrew Jackson, and that the nation is on the verge of ruin. He even insists that the corn does not grow as high as it did when he was a boy, and says the Mississippi River is filling up and will soon spread out, cover all the plantations with mud and then dry up."

Our informant had gotten this far when she was interrupted by a loud, petulant exclamation from Mr. Spears on the gallery, while he dropped both his heels on the floor with a resounding thwack.

"Just as I expected," he groaned," "What on earth is to become of us?"

"What's the matter now, husband?" said a good humored voice farther down the gallery.

"Everything's the matter," said the worried

looking man, referring again to his paper. "Here on the first page is an account of how the big trees in California are being rapidly destroyed, and on the second page an article telling of the rapid and wholesale disappearance of the pine forests in the South by the sawmills and turpentine business. Why, wife, there soon won't be a tree left."

"Yes, I read the article before you did," she replied soothingly, "and when you read farther, you will notice that the writer admits that while what he says is true, yet so vast are these forests that it will take several centuries to entirely denude the land, and you know that you and I will not be here then."

"That may be so," replied Mr. Spears, looking a little appeased, "but there is our posterity; what's to become of them?"

"Oh," said the cheerful wife, "don't you worry about your posterity. They will take care of themselves."

Here Mr. Spears resumed his paper, indulging now and then, as he read, in sudden snorts, and loud pooh-poohs, and grumbling comments, that sounded not very much unlike a dog snarling and worrying over a bone.

Finally the wife said soothingly to him:

"Mr. Spears, lay aside your paper awhile and take a walk down town. It will do you good."

"I can go," he replied, "but it won't do me any good, for the whole town is going to the Old Scratch as fast as it can."

And so growling and grumbling about ballot boxes being stuffed, and miners not getting their rights, and whitecaps not being put down, and the Chinese and Hawaiians and Filipinos filling the whole country and no room left for a white man, Mr. Spears got up and stalked down the street, hitting the bricks with his walking cane as if he wanted to break every one of them.

After he left, we were introduced to Mrs. Spears, a good, comfortable soul of fifty years or more.

On expressing our regrets that Mr. Spears had found so much to be worried about in the papers that morning, she laughed a rich, merry laugh, and said :

"It is not just this morning, but every morning with my husband. He has changed his papers twenty times, but still continues to read them ; has joined four different churches, and belonged to three different parties, Republican, Democrat and Populist. He is now thinking of going back to the Republican party."

After a few more words with Mrs. Spears, who had all unconsciously aroused our profoundest sympathy, we said to her:

"Will you deliver a message to your husband from me?"

"Certainly," she replied.

"Tell him," we continued, "that what he needs is a good case of regeneration, followed immediately by the blessing of entire sanctification, that if he gets these, he will ever after feel all right, whether the world is right or not."

*   *   *   *   *

Two years from that morning, we met Mr. Spears for the third time. He was at a Holiness Camp Meeting and was standing on his feet testifying. His face was all aglow, his voice rang out with holy fervor, and we scarcely could recognize him as the same man. His wife sat near him as he spoke and she looked to be brimming over with joy. We heard this much of his testimony. He said:

"I was the most miserable man that walked the earth. I worried about everything, and found fault with everybody. I marvel how my dear wife here managed to stand me. I wonder somebody didn't kill me for being so contrary.

"Well, one day my wife told me that a preacher had left a message for me. I snapped out, 'What is it?' She said he requested me to say to you that you needed a good case of regeneration, and then a clear experience of entire sanctification.

"Somehow that message went into my heart like an arrow. I said, if a stranger sees I need two things, I must be bad off.

"Of course I fussed about it, and called the message a piece of impertinence, but I could not get rid of the words. They put me in the way of salvation thinking, and salvation getting. I made some big mistakes at first, and thought it was water baptism I wanted; but my wife told me I had been sprinkled when I was a baby, that she heard my mother say so. Well, then, I said I wanted to be sprinkled as a man; what does a baby know about baptism? So I was re-baptized. Still I felt no better.

"At last a Baptist preacher met me and told me what I needed was to go UNDER the water. So down I went and came up in the Baptist Church, but still I had this gnawing, worried, restless, unsatisfied feeling here. Then somebody told me that there was a man in Chicago who believed in Triune Immersion, and so I took the train, made application, and went under the water three times, and came up in still another church. Wife there, bless her heart, went with me, not only to Chicago, but under the water, and under three times. I verily believe that woman would have made a didapper duck of herself, a regular mermaid, to have helped me to get right.''

Here we looked at Mrs. Spears, who was covered with pleased smiles, as with a garment, and was beaming on her husband.

"In spite of all this," continued Mr. Spears, "I did not feel satisfied. I began to remember that the third time I went under the water my right shoulder was not entirely covered, and was thinking of going up to Chicago and having the whole thing done over, when I heard there was a big Holiness Camp Meeting to take place on this ground. This was a year ago. I came because I was miserable and didn't know what else to do. Then I had some curiosity, from all the reports I had heard, about the Holiness people.

"Some of you will remember how I came to that altar the very first night for salvation, and how I got it on the third day. Then, you remember, I commenced seeking for entire sanctification. The preacher had said I needed two things, and now I know it. Thank God, on the last night of the meeting, after six days' seeking with prayers, tears, groans and faith in Christ, God gloriously sanctified my soul. You all saw me, and heard me, too, that night.

"The instant I got it, I felt that that was what I had been wanting all my life. For one year I have lived not only in Canaan, but in Heaven. I feel the glory in my soul all the time. I can hardly keep from hollering on the street. I went to a small town the other day on business, where I didn't know a soul, but I met an old negro and took him aside and told him I was sanctified. We both shouted behind a blacksmith shop.

"Ugly as I am, when I look in the glass it seems I am getting good looking. My wife there looks like she is sixteen years old. The crops look better this year than I ever saw them in all my life, and the apples taste sweeter. I believe the world is getting better every day, and I don't see what there is to keep back the millennium. Glory to God, I am saved, sanctified and satisfied. The blessing in my soul is getting richer, sweeter and bigger every day. I don't see how I can hold any more. Thank God, Jesus lives in my soul all the time, and I am at last a happy man."

XXI.

A SALVATION EPISODE.

A FEW years since the writer was on a train in a southern State going to one of his appointments. He was passing down the aisle, when a lady stopped him and said :

" Is not this Dr. C.? "

" Yes, madam."

" I thought so," she continued, " from a picture I have seen of you in one of your books."

She then told me that she lived in the State of A——, several hundred miles away, and was a traveling agent in a money making business ; that a few days before she was out on one of her business trips and heard on the cars that I was holding a Holiness meeting in Meridian, Mississippi ; that she was struck with the name " Holiness," and as a Christian she felt sufficiently interested to determine to stop off and hear me.

On going up into town, she discovered that the special services had closed some days before. She was greatly disappointed, but under the providence of God was thrown the same day into the com-

pany of two ladies, who, hearing her express her
regret that she had arrived too late to attend the
meeting and get the instruction on the subject, informed her to her great joy that they themselves
had obtained the blessing, and if she would go
home with them, they would do what they could
to lead her into the blessing.

She spent three days at the home of one of these
women of God, and the visit resulted in her receiving clearly and powerfully the blessing of sanctification.

Then she continued :

·· Hearing that you were about to hold another
meeting in this State, I determined to give up my
business trip, lucrative as it is, and go down to
Vicksburg and hear you preach there, and find out
all I can about what I have got, and get estab-
lished in the doctrine and experience. So I have
written to my husband in A—— what I have done,
that I have given up my trip and gone to hear you
for ten days or two weeks in Vicksburg.

"In fact," she added, "I am on the way
now, as I understand you open up there to-mor-
row."

I told the bright, happy-faced woman that I
was glad to hear the good news of herself, and

felt assured that the services would prove a great blessing to her.

In parting from her at the depot, she said :

" I know when my husband receives my letter he will think I have lost my mind."

Sure enough he did, and on the next day Mrs. S. met me on the street and showed me a telegram from her husband, which read :

" Stay in Vicksburg until I arrive."

The woman's face was radiant as she showed me the dispatch, and said :

" This is just what I wanted and was praying for. My husband is an unconverted man, and I crave to see him saved in your meeting."

On the following day, in the morning service, I saw a gentleman sitting by the side of my new friend, Mrs. S., and supposed at once and correctly that it was her husband. After dismissal, she brought him forward and introduced him, when I said in acknowledgment :

" I am glad to see you, Mr. S., and you must allow me to congratulate you on having a sanctified wife."

Mr. S.'s face immediately became a study at this remark, but prominent was a bored, skeptical and disgusted look.

In a couple of days Mr. S., who at first arrival saw that his wife's mind was all right, got to listening with increasing interest and conviction to the sermons, and at last came to the altar and was soundly converted to God.

For two or three days it was a pleasure to see his face, all illumined with the new love and life upon which he had entered. I could but rejoice to see how things had been so overruled by the providence of God as to hook this distant soul by the bait of a false alarm and reel him to the shore, and put him on that ever increasing string of redeemed ones.

But in a little while the deeper Gospel of a pure heart, or holiness, began to break in and take hold of the man, and one morning we saw his face overspread with gloom and an expression come up dark and forbidding. As the congregation was dispersing at the close of the service, Mrs. S. passed me in the aisle and hurriedly whispered:

" Get hold of God for Mr. S. Something is the matter with him, but he will not tell me what it is. I am sure that it is something that God wants him to do, and he is running from it. He says he is going home on the train at midnight. Join with me in prayer and ask God to keep him from going.

It will never do for him to leave at this time.   He must get sanctified now.   Everything depends upon it.''

The woman's eyes were full of tears as she turned from me and vanished in the crowd.

Of course I '' held on,'' as the wife had requested, while she, knowing more than I did about the man and how much was involved in his full salvation, made every breath a prayer.

To all appearances our prayers were in vain, for at 11 o'clock that night Mr. S. began to pack his valise, and half an hour later, in spite of the tears and protests of his wife, he descended the stairs, walked out on the pavement and soon his departing footsteps died away upon the ear.

But still his wife prayed on, saying,

'' Lord, do not let him be able to get aboard the train.   Prevent him by your power some way and bring him back.''

At 1 o'clock as she lay wakeful upon the bed, she heard his step coming slowly and heavily up the stairs, the door open, the valise drop on the floor, and Mr. S. himself sink down in a chair as if he was made of lead.   In a minute he spoke to the silent but expectant wife.

'' I could not get off.   Every time I put my foot

on the car step, some strange power seemed to pull it down and draw me back."

The room was dark, and the man's face was scarcely less dark or gloomy, but there was one bright countenance in that room and one thankful heart that had already begun to praise God inwardly for answered prayer.

The next day the wife saw that a terrible conflict was going on in her husband's breast. She felt it best not to question him, and he did not offer to explain, only dropping the words that he had something to do back in the town where he lived that would kill him to perform.

She tried to encourage him, but being ignorant of the trouble that oppressed him, she was at a great disadvantage; besides he was not in a mood to be encouraged.

Late that afternoon, and before the regular preaching service, we held our usual prayer meeting in a class-room of the church. About twenty people were present. Mr. S. was present with his wife. He was kneeling back of the writer and several feet away. The presence of the Holy Ghost was very graciously and powerfully felt, and the writer was leading in prayer. He was repeating the words of Christ, "Father, sanctify them," when a voice cried out in most thrilling accents,

" I will do it, Lord!" When, crash! we heard a human form fall on the floor.

Glancing around, we saw Mr. S. stretched out full length, and looking upward with hands clasped and face covered with happy smiles. He had received the blessing of sanctification in the very moment of crying out, " I will do it, Lord."

In explanation of it all, it seems that a year or so before a prominent man in the town where he lived had in some way offended Mr. S., and so one night he went around to that gentleman's house near the hour of twelve with the full intention of calling him to the door and shooting him down. By some merciful providence of God the deed was prevented. Moreover, at our meeting our friend had repented and obtained forgiveness for the spirit of murder that had been entertained in his heart. But when he commenced seeking the blessing of sanctification, the Lord recalled the occurrence to him and said,

" Are you willing to write to this man and tell him how you intended to kill him at midnight at his own door, and how I have saved you from it all?"

Here then commenced the struggle in the breast

of Mr. S., just as it comes to all who seek holiness,
for God puts severe tests of obedience to all who
want the pearl of great price. No man can obtain
the grace unless he says yes to every command of
the Lord. Hence the tests alluded to on the line
of perfect, unquestioning obedience. With some,
He puts a number of demands. With the person of
whom we are writing, the main and crushing ex-
action was a written confession to the man whom
he had intended to shoot.

Sometimes people overlook the full divine design in a confession like the one mentioned above.
It works a double purpose. It tests the sincerity
and faithfulness of the seeker after holiness, and it,
so to speak, breaks to pieces the man to whom the
admission is made. So the acknowledgment
is tremendously effective at both ends of the
line.

Anyhow, it brought about a death struggle with
Mr. S. He tried to fight off the impression, but it
would not leave. He then endeavored to argue it
away, but it would not be convinced. He then
pleaded with God about it.

"Why, Lord, I will not be able to look the man
in the face when I return home."

"Will you do as I bid you?"

" But, Lord, the whole town will look on me as a cut-throat and assassin, and I will be ruined."

" Will you obey me?"

And so the spiritual battle raged, the Devil tormented, God quietly but steadily urged perfect obedience, and the face of the unhappy man became dark, stern and forbidding.

Now then came the determination to imitate Jonah and run from God, and then the announcement to his wife that he was going to return home that night on the midnight train.

The reader knows the rest—how two of us got hold of God to keep him from leaving, how he felt a strange power hindering him from boarding the train, how he stalked back to his room at one o'clock, came to the afternoon meeting, and suddenly yielding to God, cried out, "I will do it, Lord!" and as suddenly was filled with the Holy Ghost and knocked flat on the floor by the power of the Almighty.

* * * *

All this happened seven years ago. Now and then we heard in regard to the brother that he was doing well in the Canaan life. Several years ago we met him and saw that the report was true. A few days since we received a letter from the wife, saying:

"Knowing your interest in Mr. S., I write to tell you that he passed away from earth to heaven this summer. It was a death of peace, triumph and rapture beyond all words to describe."

In the light of this small portion of the letter we see more than ever that in the comings and goings of our lives, the meetings here and happenings there, God comes and with His blessed overruling, directing and shaping power brings out the most unexpected and yet blessed of results. In the case we have just considered, a rumor of a revival meeting, and a conversation on the train, brought regeneration to one soul, sanctification to two, and glorification since then to the subject of this sketch.

XXII.

BITTER PILLS.

IN the swamp country of the Land of Dixie, a disease is generated among its sloughs and low grounds called "The Chills." This malady is known to be the result of malaria taken into the system. One curious feature of the sickness is, that while one hour the victim feels he is freezing, the next he is burning up. A second feature is a violent shaking of the body and chattering of the teeth, both of which are perfectly uncontrollable while the ague is at its height. So serious are these shakings that it only requires a few returns of the same to loosen a man's hold on this world and throw him into another. A third remarkable feature is that the day following the first chill, and generally called "the second day," seems to be a resting time granted by nature to the sufferer, that he might have a chance to recuperate and rally his forces before the disease appears again to give him another push toward the grave. This aforesaid "second day" is also the medicine or dosing day, for if quinine is not promptly and sufficiently introduced so as to compel the bacteria to get out of the blood or loosen their hold on certain inner membranes, then there is certain to come on the third day another victory for the chills, with higher fever, greater freezings, and all the accompanying chatterings, shiverings and shakings, that belong to the malady.

In some way, as a lad of fifteen, we had received the malaria, and was brought down full length and helpless upon the bed. We had frozen, burned up, shook, and trembled until we were perfectly worn out. We were so tired of the shaking that we would not have protested a second if some one would have suggested laying a cotton bale on us instead of a blanket. We had discovered "perpetual motion," and perfectly satisfied, not to say sick of the discovery, were ready to part with the secret for anything or nothing. It was wearing us out, who had found it, even as it had broken others down who were seeking it. It was too wonderful for us. We wanted no more of it.

After this came the "second day," in which the physical system rested and gathered itself for another earthquake to begin on schedule time the next morning with premonitory gapings, stretchings, sighings and tossings on the bed.

Pale, weak, dispirited, we looked forth on the world from the depths of a pillow and discovered a form standing by the bedside. We studied the phenomenon dreamily and observed that the size was medium, color, black, and sex, female.

We also noticed a glass of water to be in one hand and a shallow, red box in the other, filled with round white things the size of a pea, and standing knee-deep in a yellowish powder. These spheres were pills, and bitter pills at that. They were quinine pills.

We shuddered at the sight. Even to this day we have shiverings at the recollection, and feel a peculiar knot or rising up in the throat, attended with unmistakable symptoms of nausea.

By and by a voice proceeded from the form :

"Here's yer pills."

I lay and wondered at such a speech. The girl spoke as if I did not know the pills were there ; just as if they had not rolled up like great dark bodies of the most solid, opaque matter, eclipsing happiness and filling all life with shadow and misery.

Then, to think of her saying they were "my pills," as though they were my peculiar property, or I wanted any such possession !

Naturally, therefore, no sign was given from the pillow or bedclothes that any such absurd speech had been heard. A perfect abstraction was counterfeited.

So the voice sounded again upon the air, solemn and sepulchral as though coming from the catacombs.

"Is yer gwine ter take dese pills?"

Our abstraction grew deeper. The knot in the throat became larger. Nausea developed. General wretchedness increased.

Again the voice:

"Is yer gwine ter take dese pills, or mus' I call yer Ma?"

At these words, and especially the last, I arose immediately and sat up in bed.

"Where are the pills?" I asked, as though suddenly interested and conscious for the first time of their proximity.

"Here dey is," replied the sphinx by my side, thrusting the pills right under my nose.

"Ugh!" I exclaimed, and shuddering, hid my face, fell back flat on the bed and begged for just one minute's respite by the clock.

It was granted, and the dark hand was withdrawn.

Then came a musing fit, which lasted five minutes ; then a fixed gazing out of the window, and
more deep thought and abstraction.

The hand of the form by the bedside commenced moving towards me again ; the voice
began :

"Is yer gwine ter take—"

"Please remove," I interrupted, "the two I
am to take from the rest. Don't bring an army
against me, but kill me by platoons." All this in
bitter irony.

Thirty seconds were gained by this piece of
strategy. But at the end of that time, there was the
black hand and that dreadful voice again, and there
was the glass of water and the pills, which seemed
by this time to have the circumference of cart
wheels, while the yellow powder in which they
stood, looking like dust, favored the idea.

And now we became suddenly and greatly interested in other things. What was that noise outside the window? Who was that talking in the
other room? Where was my hat? Had my brother
gone to school? Had my horse, Lightfoot, been
fed?

The answers were only too quickly given.
There was no one outside the window. It was my

mother in the other room. My brother had gone to school. The horse had been fed, and would I take the pills or must she call my—

" Where is the water?"

" Here it is."

" Have you got a piece of ham?"

" Yes."

" Got some jelly?"

" Yes."

" Is the foot tub there?"

Yes, everything is there, and all things are ready indeed, except the boy.

Then came a glance at the pills, and then a hurried looking away. They seemed to be growing larger all the while.

But what need to dwell on the long hour spent in advancing towards and retreating from these globes of trouble, the arousing and sinking back, the clenching and the unclenching of the teeth, the taking up one of the pills in the hand as if weighing it, and then—laying it back in the box, while the body shuddered and the bowed head shook negatively from side to side as much as to say, it can not be done !

What need to dwell on the periodic, oracular like utterance by my side from the black servant.

" Here's yer pills. Is you gwine ter take yer pills?"

How shall I describe the arrangements for battle and the last struggle? The piece of ham is before me, the spoon of jelly in reach, a lump of sugar and slice of apple hard by. Beyond, there are the towel and foot tub.

What need to say that the first pill was bitten in two ; that another all covered with jelly came out of the sweet encircling, the preserves going down all right and the pill remaining in the mouth all wrong.

At last, after being exhorted, entreated, commanded, threatened, I, with one great gulp, swallowed two. One of the couple remained clinging with its hands to the side of the throat beyond the reach of the finger. As for the other, its locality farther down was as well known as any piece of furniture in the room. Are not all these things written in the chronicles of the family?

Well, the pills, with a dozen others, were swallowed in due time, and their health-restoring property realized. The bitter became sweet. Sickness gave way to better conditions, and I arose from the bed, and live today because of the aforesaid bitter medicine.

*   *   *   *

Oh the bitter pills of this life! Who has not had to take them? There are diseases of the soul as well as of the body. There is such a thing as unhealthfulness of the spirit. The conscience and heart can get wrong. The character may be hurt.

At such a time, so far as religious usefulness is concerned, the man is profitless. He becomes one of the many invalids in the church. The sparkle has gone from the eye, the light from the face and the spring from the step. Virtually he is in bed; there can be no question about that.

The reader will remember that right then and there certain bitter pills were offered him. They were just as real and unavoidable as though a dark form stood by and with relentless hand pressed them to the lips.

Let us look at the box and see the names of these pills, and study the character of the medicine. Apologies, that a Christian law and spirit demand, should be made; acts of restitution and reparation for deeds and words that have been hurtful to others; or it is a private confession of a private wrong; or a public acknowledgment of an open misdeed; or it is a humiliating position under God's providence that has to be occupied; or some defect or failure in a life work which has to be accepted.

The reader knows the pills well. How strange it is that men fail to realize the benefit of their bitter qualities, upon the pride-engorged and sin-sick heart.

Can the reader ever forget how he coquetted, so to speak, with those pills ; how he looked, and refused to look again ; how he hid his face, shuddered, sickened, and said he could never take them —that it was impossible?

We get a little closer and talk in the second person, singular number.

Do you remember, my reader, that all this while there seemed to be within you or near you a dark, sorrowful Presence in whose eyes shone the light of calm judgment and who kept whispering:

"This is your medicine—will you take it?"

Do you remember how long you refused to hear that voice ; how you counterfeited abstraction with your conscience? How you tried to become absorbed in other matters, and how you thought and asked, and lived a thousand foolish things? How you tried to become interested in other and outside affairs, and how you utterly failed because of that immovable hand which still presented the bitter, nauseous potion of an unmistakable duty?

You noticed that you got no better. The conviction grew that you had to take the pills to be well with man and God.

Then came the idea of dividing the pill, then the plan of making it more palatable by coating it with jelly : or to speak literally, you made efforts to obtain concession from the other side. Or the jelly happened to be a half confession, or a misleading confession.

It was all in vain. The hand was never withdrawn. The voice continued to say :

" There are your pills. Will you take them?"

You even insisted after all this that you were not sick, that there was nothing in the world the matter with you. But the symptoms of disease were unmistakable—a coated tongue, feeble pulse, weak action of the heart, a listless, heavy feeling, loss of appetite, shooting pains, nervous fears and apprehensions by day and bad dreams at night. Yes, there was no doubt about it, you were sick.

*   *   *   *

The best and only thing to do is to take the pills. The reader will remember that he had rebelled against God's will in some circumstance of life, and then had to bow to and accept the will. Or you had wronged some man or woman in purse, character or reputation, and you felt impressed to undo the wrong. You had spoken harshly and untruly of some individual, and it had to be recalled. You had sinned publicly against Christ and the Church, and there was an open confession of the wrong to be made. These were some of the pills, and the Word, Spirit and Providence of God agreed that you had to take them.

You said at the time that it was so hard to do this. But in like manner those pills were difficult to swallow in the days of my boyhood; but I took them and got well!

You replied that you had made a number of efforts, but they all ended in failure; that you opened your lips to make the confession, started to beg forgiveness, made a movement toward righting some wrong of the past, but broke down. In a word, you took up the pill, fully intending to swallow it, but it looked so large, was so dreadfully bitter, that you laid it down again. And so you remained sick.

But the day came—can you ever forget it—when you made up your mind to do the just, right, and

Christ-like thing. You heard the call of duty and answered, " Here am I." You took up your cross. You squared life and heart for the peculiar burden. You accepted your providential situation. You made confession and reparation. In a word you took the pills.

Now what! Behold an instantaneous, delicious sense of spiritual health rushed into you. Moral disease fled, and light, strength and gladness entered. Since then there has been a thrilling experience of a most wholesome soundness. The medicine was bitter, but the cure under God and through Christ was wonderful. You are now well, and face, voice, eye and life prove it.

Believe me, my readers, who have not done this, that the thing you need most is not the sugar plum of a false consolation, but the bitter pills which God has been presenting you a long time through some dark and sorrowful convictions of duty. You will never be well until you take them.

You know well what those pills are, and have been knowing for months and years. I have translated their names from a spiritual Materia Medica. They are long and hard to pronounce, but by poring over them they can be understood. Here are a few,

" Pleaseforgivemewife."

" Iwantyoutopardonmehusband,"

" Iwastoohastyandseverewithyoumychild."

" MybrotherIhavewrongedyouandaskyourforgi-veness."

" Hereisasumofmoneythatbelongstoyouneighbo-rIrestoreitandbegyoutoforgiveme."

Varied have been the experiences of people with these pills. The soul is convinced that they should be taken, but who is naturally inclined to do such a thing?

So men have cut them in two, bitten them in two, or one was chewed instead of being swallowed. A third slipped out of the jelly coating and caused much gagging. And still another stuck in the throat.

O the inward and outward protest against these pills; the nausea they create; the excuses for not being taken they have caused to be invented!

And so the health of the daughter of my people was not recovered.

But at last you took the pills in your hand, put them squarely in your mouth, threw your head back like a man, fixed your eyes upon the heavens, and taking a big gulp of the water of life—down they went!

Since then, what? You have been a well man! You took up your bed, so to speak, and walked! Light is in your eyes, health in your soul, and strength in your life. You have left the hospital and resumed business at the old stand. But it looks somehow like a new stand; the sign seems to have been repainted and the owner appears to be rejuvenated, if not re-created. And besides all this, there seems to be a greater rush of Christian business there than was ever known before.

Anyhow, the sick man is well.

XXIII.

A TRYING EXPERIENCE.

THREE youths were in attendance upon a Southern college. They belonged to one of the Secret Societies that usually are found among the young men of these places of education. The fraternity of which they were members was the most mysterious of all the other secret clubs, and fairly luxuriated in their reputation of nerve-trying initiations, remote and spectral meetings in the woods, in the burning of different colored lights during their sessions, and strange, weird calls to one another, that were only understood by themselves.

It became necessary for this Secret Society to obtain possession of a human skull, and information reaching them in a private way that a lonely, neglected and almost forgotten graveyard was in the woods a mile southwest of the college, the Grand Mogul of this mysterious fraternity appointed three of its members to go forth after 12 o'clock on the first moonless night and secure a skull from one of the graves.

The youths thus selected for the trying work we

will call A——, C—— and H——, their ages being eighteen, nineteen and twenty-two. H—— was the oldest.

According to agreement they crept quietly out of their respective dormitories while the large college clock in the belfry of the main building was tolling out the solemn notes of twelve. Like three shadows they flitted beneath the great trees of the campus, and met at the stile on the south side of the grounds. They spoke in whispers, and glancing back, observed that every light was extinguished in the college buildings. Even M——, the hardest student among the five hundred, had gone to bed.

On taking a silent inventory, A—— had a spade, C—— had secured a dark lantern, and H——, who wore a light overcoat and had a small bundle under it, said it was a towel and soap to wash at the branch after the exhumation, and that he also carried under his arm, wrapped up, a pistol.

C—— asked him what good it would do to shoot at ghosts.

H——snickered and said, noise laid spirits if it did nothing more; that anyhow he felt safer with the firearms.

After these short whisperings the three boys

slipped over the stile, gained the high road, and
after a walk of three quarters of a mile through a
field and then some shadowy woods, crossed a
dark branch at the foot of a hill, where they were to
wash their hands from the defilements of the grave.
It was a gloomy ravine and the low, gurgling sound
of the water coming out of and disappearing in the
darkness was anything but reassuring. It had a
strangling sound, and the boys wiped their faces
and felt a most decided and rapid increase of the
action of their hearts.

Ascending the hill beyond, they came to its
forest covered brow, and after a few yards saw in
the dim starlight the left hand fork, which, much
fainter than the main road, led away to the graveyard they were seeking. The woods here became
at once much thicker and wilder, as they left the
highway, and they were compelled to light the
dark lantern.

H—— was left at the junction of the two roads
to watch and give any needed alarm. This was
his own suggestion, and A—— and C—— opposed
it and insisted that he should watch at the edge of
the graveyard. But H—— said it was barely a fur-
long distant and this was the strategic point to
guard and protect them, either by firing the pistol

to give them warning of interruption, or by stepping down the road quickly to where they were digging and give the alarm.

A—— and C—— were both now inwardly convinced that H—— had weakened and was a coward. So they left him with mixed feelings, and, turning their lantern light up, pushed carefully along the dark road, which was made all the darker by the small glimmering lamp, as it actually intensified the shadows, and caused the great tree trunks to appear more spectral and solemn than they did in the starlight.

They could hear the dripping of the dew as it fell from the leaves to the turf below. Then the woods would heave a sigh as if in unrest and sorrow about something. Once a great night bird almost swept their faces with his broad wings as he beat his startled way swiftly from them and vanished with a rustling sound in the tree tops. A screech owl with its sudden, startling cry made their hearts leap into their throats for a moment, and some kind of small animal of the forest gave them another shock as it rushed away through the underbrush at the sound of their steps.

Several times they thought they heard footsteps following them, but remembering that H——

was standing guard at the head of the road, and also failing to see anyone or anything on stopping and turning their light backward, they felt reassured and pushed on.

At last, after traversing a distance of fully three hundred yards from the main public road, they found themselves stumbling over headboards and into sunken graves, and knew they had reached the place they sought.

There was considerable uncertainty about this graveyard, both at college and in town. Some said a battle had been fought there during the Civil War, and a number of soldiers had been buried in the woods by the side of this faint country road. Others said that the bodies of citizens, as well as soldiers, who had died in a large hospital up town, were interred here. There was still another report, but the facts were that here in the woods by the side of a faint trail or path, and several hundred yards from the highway, was a hundred graves all overshadowed with the great trees of a forest and almost hidden by a smaller growth springing up around and upon the graves.

A—— and C—— selected a grave near the road, mainly, we suppose, with a view to keep their communications open toward civilization. A small opening in the trees allowed a little starlight to fall upon the head board and upper portion of the mound, but the lower part was in dense shadow from an unusually large and thick tree that flung its boughs over it.

The lads lost no time in getting to work, and while one held the lantern, the other wielded the spade, and began to cast out the earth. They alternated with the work, and in one of their short resting spells they heard the college clock toll the hour of one. It sounded so faint, far away and solemn that they wished they had not heard it. After this they heard nothing more for several minutes but the hoot of a distant owl and the melancholy cry of a whippoorwill.

They both worked when handling the spade with all their strength, for they were anxious to get through and be gone. Then the night wind gave an occasional sigh as if sorry at what they were doing, and the dropping of the dew from the branches sounded like the drip of blood.

They had reached a depth of three feet, and C—— was in the grave, when in the act of pressing his foot on the spade, the whole thing under him caved in and he sank almost out of sight from A——,who sat squatted with the lamp in his hand on the ground above. The shock to C—— was terriffic, though he went down only three feet, yet to him it felt and seemed a thousand. To add to the horror, he landed on the head of the dead man, or more truly speaking, the skull of the skeleton.

C—— clambered out up to A—— with a celerity that was remarkable, bathed in a cold sweat and exceedingly agitated. The lads discussed the happening in whispers, and saw that the man had not been buried in a coffin, but in a large box fully three feet deep; that the lid or top had not sunken in during the past years, for there was no pressure upon it until C——'s full weight, with the entering spade had broken through the decayed plank and let him down suddenly into the bottom of the grave and in the midst of the bones.

After a while C—— crept back into the grave, and feeling around in the dark, found the skull, caught it in his left hand and standing erect, started to climb out. Just then A—— gave an exclamation of horror, and in a low, startled voice said to C——.

" Just look yonder !''

C—— quickly turned and there, near the foot of the grave, stood a white form. In another second the figure stretched out an arm and said in a low, blood-curdling tone,

" Let my bones alone !"

How C—— got out of the grave he never knew, only that in a single second he was out dashing for the road, but still holding to the skull.

A—— had flung his lamp away in his terror, and was now speeding with all his might for the main road and college. C——, in endeavoring to follow him, tripped over a small tree lying in his path and tumbled over and over on the ground in one direction, while the skull, struck from his hand by the violence of the fall, rolled in another.

It would have been impossible to have found it in the dark, and C——, knowing that it would be unkind as well as disregardful of the rights of the true owner of the skull to try to obtain it again, and feeling that it was his duty to assist A—— in getting at once out of the woods, and not allow him to have that long, lonely run to the college entirely without companionship, and recognizing a great increasing, inward craving for the sight of human habitations and the presence of living beings who wore their own skulls, gathered himself together and struck out after A—— with the greatest singleness of mind and doubleness of strength.

As they came panting to the junction of the two roads, H—— was not to be seen. They were convinced, as they had suspected before, that he was a coward and had slunk back to college and left them with the whole job, and now the whole terror on their hands.

Under healthy and proper conditions neither A—— nor C—— believed in ghosts or supernatural appearances. But nearly a mile from college, in the woods, with the ghostly happening in the graveyard still blistering the memory, they were not in the mental frame to speak coolly and deliberately upon the subject. They felt more like running than anything else, and so with an intense desire to be close to actual living folks again, they swept into the public road, flew down the slope of the hill, leaped the little branch that was still strangling and choking in the darkness, and pantingly sped up the ascent on the other side, A—— still leading and C—— closely following.

The boys reached the College at last, and as they pulled themselves over the stile felt, from the nervous shock and the run of a mile without stopping, that they were more dead than alive.

Creeping to one of the pumps, they quietly washed their hands and bathed their crimson faces, drank copious draughts of the pure, cool fluid, and then stole away to their rooms.

On meeting H—— next day, A—— and C—— were at first very cool and dignified, which he returned with interest. They, then, taking him aside, demanded to know why he forsook his post and left them in the lurch.

To their surprise he warmly and firmly denied having left them, but said a man had gone by his post where he was concealed, and he had walked forty or fifty yards up the public road to see if he had gone on, and was returning to his position by the forks of the road when he saw A—— and C—— coming out of the woods and flying down the highway like the Devil was after them ; that he supposed it was a trick to leave him alone in the woods, and that he had followed them back to College slowly and feeling justly offended.

A—— and C—— had before promised each other to say nothing of the startling apparition at the grave, feeling that no one would believe them, that every boy would laugh at them, and H—— would tease them continually and unmercifully. So they replied that they did not intend to leave him in the forest alone, but they fancied they were discovered at the grave by some midnight prowler and had fled, and that not finding H—— at the forks of the road, they naturally supposed he had forsaken them and gone back to the college.

H—— seemed somewhat pacified at this, but tried to get A—— and C—— to describe more explicity their interruption. Was it a young or old man? Was he small or large? Did he say anything or not?

To these questions the two friends answered that they did not stop to examine the intruder, they only knew that they were discovered by somebody who came upon them in the midst of their work, and that knowing if they were found out they would be punished, both by the College Faculty and town officials, they had simple skedaddled.

To the repeated question, Did he say anything to you, their reply was, "only enough for us to know he knew what we were doing."

H—— had to be satisfied with this, for he could get nothing more out of the two boys.

A week later the local paper contained an item, which created a buzz for some days, both in the town and college. It read as follows:

"While Mr. Montague, our County Surveyor, was running a line near the old graveyard a mile south of the College, he discovered that one of the graves had been recently opened. He found a spade in the grave, a dark lantern a few feet distant, a small piece of white cloth hanging on a thorn bush, and thirty or forty feet away a human skull. He with his two men replaced the skull in the grave, threw the dirt back and replanted the head board. But to him as well as to us the affair is shrouded in mystery. Why should the grave be opened? Why should the lantern and spade be left? And if these disturbers of the dead wanted the skull, why should they go to all the pains to get it out, and then cast it away? It is to be hoped that these transgressors will be brought to light and properly punished."

A——, C—— and H—— together could have answered most of these questions, but it was to their interest not to do so, and so the talk died away and the circumstance ceased to be thought of by the public.

It was a long time, however, before A—— and C—— slept soundly through a whole night. Both had distressing dreams, and had only to close their eyes, after their room lamps were extinguished at night, to see a white figure and hear a low, grating voice saying, "Let my bones alone."

*   *   *   *

The three boys of this sketch left college the the same year. A—— was a brilliant fellow and would have distinguished himself in the profession he chose, but he died just one year after leaving the university. C——, after a few years, entered the ministry and was sent to a distant great city. H—— became a prominent lawyer and was made a judge.

Something like ten or fifteen years after they left college, one day C——received a letter from H——. It was quite short, but it had a tremendous effect on the reader. It ran thus:

> Dear C——,
>
> " Let my bones alone."
>
> H——.

It was a perfect study to watch the countenance of C——. No pen description could do justice to the varying expressions that rapidly followed each other over his face. Astonishment and wonder of mind, twitching of mouth, pulling at moustache, biting of lips, a curious sparkle in the eye, with a part dazed, part ashamed, part vexed and part amused look, all striving together in a most wonderful manner on the same countenance. In fact,

for a while it was difficult to say what would be the
final outcome and lasting expression. Of course
there would be a survival of the fittest, but which
was the fittest?

The next mail carried C——'s reply :
Dear H——.

   You old rascal you! I wish I was in
arm's length of your body, and verily you should
have better cause than once before to say, " Let my
bones alone ! " This time you would have positive
need to say it, for on this occasion I would not let
your bones alone. You surely belong to the Bonaparte family. Anyhow you were in the past a supernatural fraud, and I gravely fear you are still a
humbug. Nevertheless, as I ran off with your
skull, of course you can not help being such things,
and so I freely forgive you.

     Your old college friend,

        C——.

XXIV.

A STRANGE VISITOR.

LET NOT the reader suppose from the caption of this chapter that strange visits and visitors are a rare occurrence to the writer. Some have been remarkable above all description, and many most unusual. But numbers were paid in strictest confidence, and in numerous cases what was said and confided was with the understanding that all was in the light and protection of a sacred confessional, and so the history of those hours will never be written by the author, and will go with him, unknown by the world, to the Judgment Day.

But the case represented in this chapter had no embargo of promised secrecy upon it, and is used, in its simple description of a morning call, as a window through which the reader can look upon a peculiar phase of that always interesting thing, a human life.

I was busily writing at my desk one afternoon, in a hotel in a certain town, when there came a tap at the door. Burdened with the thought of several chapters to write to complete an unfinished book, an article to pen for one of the religious papers, and a great pile of unanswered letters before me, I glanced up from my work with a sigh, and said :

" Come in."

The door opened and a plain looking man of about forty, having the appearance of a farmer, entered. Closing the door behind him, he drew near several paces and made a peculiar bow, with one hand resting upon his knee and bending sideways. With an earnest face and grave voice he said :

" I hope you will excuse me, sir, but I want to see you, for I am in trouble."

The word " trouble " was sufficient to banish my last regret at being disturbed in my work, and I said kindly to him :

" Take a seat, sir, and tell me what I can do for you."

He placed his hat on the floor between his feet, and looking fixedly at me with a pair of melancholy black eyes, said :

" I hate to interrupt you, sir, for I know you must be a busy man, but I felt drawn to come. I want you to dissolve a great mystery for me. Will you answer me some questions?"

" I do not know that I can, but I will try," was my reply.

" Well, I am a man who sees sights. They come to me. Now what I want to know is, is it the sympathy of the flesh, or the substance of the spirit?"

" I don't think I understand your last remark," I said.

The man repeated the words exactly, rubbing his chin reflectively with his hand, while inclining his body toward me and fixing on me a most anxious look.

" Who is it you see?" I inquired.

" My wife. She is dead and in her grave, but appears to me every twenty-four hours." And the man's eyes filled with tears.

" My dear sir," I replied, " I do not believe such appearances are actual or real, but arise from one's own mental condition. They spring from your own fancy."

" Fancy!" exclaimed the man scornfully. "Why, sir, I hold her in my arms."

" Still, I can not but think, " said I, " that your constant thought of your wife creates the impression or vision which you regard as a reality."

" It is a reality," replied the man warmly, " and I came here hoping you would dissolve the mystery. I am an ignorant man, never had any schooling, and hoped you could help me."

" I don't see," I answered, " what I can do for you : for granting that it is a real manifestation or spiritual appearance, the Bible forbids any effort on our part to hold communion with the spirit world, or the dead."

" But they come to me," cried the man, getting up out of his chair. " But I won't disturb you any more." and he started for the door.

" A feeling of profound pity for the bereaved man swept over my heart and caused me to say gently and kindly to him.

" How long has your wife been dead? "

" Just forty-three days. And oh how I loved her ! You never saw such a woman, straight as an arrow and fine-looking, and everybody said she had the finest figure they ever saw."

" And you say she comes back to you?"

" Yes sir. The night after the funeral she woke me up calling me, and as I opened my eyes, I saw her standing by the bed. ' What's the matter, dear,' I said. And she said, ' I am cold,' and crept into bed with me, and I took the cover and wrapped it round her and drew her to my heart. Oh, how I love her !"

There was a minute's silence, in which the man

seemed to labor for breath and looked as if his heart would break. Then he resumed,

" She kept coming to me night after night, till I felt something must be wrong, and one night she told me something about her body. So the next day I hired a man to go to the graveyard with me, and we dug her up."

" How did she look? "

" Oh her face was peaceful, but what she had told me about her body was just as she said," **and** the man related things that we do not repeat.

" What did you do then?"

" I put all the flowers back in the coffin with her, and reburied her."

" And does she still return?"

" Yes, every twenty-four hours," and the man's face was a study with its expression of mingled suffering and joy. " Sometimes when I see her she is in one place, and next time in another. Not long ago I saw her one night and she seemed to be in a foreign country, and appeared to be another man's wife ; but I went right up and took hold of her. O how I love her ! "

At this the man buried his face in his hands, and I could see the tears trickling through the closed fingers. After a pause of fully a couple of minutes, in which not a word was spoken on either side, and I heard a church bell ringing in the distance, he lifted his face and said,

" I saw her again last night, and she was leading a child by the hand. Her head was drooped so that I could not see her face, but I knew it was her. Oh, I always know her! And I went straight up to her and put my arms around her."

There was no questioning the man's genuineness. The honest face, clear, truthful eyes, dripping tears, and unmistakable sorrow forbade any idea of trickery or deception of any kind.

" Sometimes," he continued, " I wonder why I was ever born, I have been through so much trouble. When I was a child, my mother was drowned in a freshet. I was a baby and was washed from the house down the stream a hundred yards, and the wind filled my little night dress and I was blown, they say, on some driftwood, where they found me. Why did God let me live to see such sorrow as has come to me since that time?"

The man's sighs and sobs were pitiful to hear.

"Then," he continued, when I was a boy, I was raised by people who nearly beat me to death. I reckon they would have killed me, but my father stole me away from them. Even then I used to have the strangest visions. One year they were awful, but after that they became beautiful and rested me like."

"Do you only see your wife?" I interrupted.

"No. Twice I have seen Christ, and I knew it was Him."

"Are you a Christian?"

"Yes, God knows I am. And yet I wonder why He let me live to see so much trouble."

"Suppose we kneel down together," I said, "and let us talk to God about it all."

So we got down on our knees side by side, and with one hand upon the shoulder of the man who wept convulsively, I commended the broken heart by me, with all its past and present burdens, to Jesus. I begged the Saviour to let Him feel that all was well with his wife, that as she had died in the faith, that her soul was with God in heaven, and her body would sleep quietly and be raised on the morning of the Resurrection. I besought the Lord to give him strength to bear up in his lonely life, and be a true, faithful Christian in his sorrow as he had been in brighter, happier days; that he might remember he owed certain duties to his children, and that he would be kind, strong and cheerful for their sakes and raise them so as to meet their mother in heaven : that He himself should be kept true through everything, until after a faithful, useful Christian life, he would rejoin his wife in the skies, and the broken ties of earth be reunited forever.

As we arose, the man had ceased his distressing sobs, and with a pathetically faint smile on his face, he grasped my hand and said,

" You are a noble man. I thank you for that prayer. It has done me so much good. My heart here don't ache so much."

" I am certainly very glad," I cordially replied, " that I have been able to help you."

"Well, indeed you have. And now, sir, goodbye. I must get back home to the children. I live four miles from town, and when I'm gone long the children miss me. They've got nobody but me now to take care of them. You ought to see them run to meet me when I come in the big gate. I take one on each shoulder and the other one rides on my back." Here he fell into a musing fit for a moment with a pleasant smile as if he was back home with his children, and then resumed :

" People round the neighborhood say I am crazy because I said I see my wife. Crazy, I say ! Can a crazy man raise first-class crops, like I do?

I make money every year. Do crazy people make money? There isn't a merchant in this town but would give me credit, and honor my orders for goods and groceries. Would they do that to crazy folks? I pay all my debts promptly. Do crazy people pay their debts? No, sir, I'm not crazy, or a fool either. But I do see those things. Goodbye, sir, I must go. The children are waiting now for me at home.''

The door closed, the footsteps died away in the hall, and my strange visitor was gone as suddenly as he had come.

I resumed my seat at my writing table, and cheek on hand, sat listening to the faint, far-off sound of the church bell that was ringing again. But it was a long time before I could call in my pensive, wandering thoughts and resume the interrupted work of my pen.

XXV.

HIGH FLOWN AFRICAN SPEECH.

THE negro, whether educated, half taught, or ignorant, is an interesting character. When by the work of schools and universities, however, he approaches the Caucasian in intelligence, culture, polish and general habits of life, the peculiar charm wielded by the untutored African personality of course disappears.

That charm, existing as it does in dialect, pronunciation, accent, mannerisms, native drollery and wit, is naturally changed, if not destroyed by the approximation of the one race to the other. So in the city negro of to-day, coming out of free school, high school and college, the peculiarities fail to appear which so impressed the observer of a preceding generation. Hence many thus confronted, will marvel over past descriptions and fail to see the place for tears and smiles once so freely accorded. For just as the Indian is disappearing under the western horizon, so the old-time negro character is vanishing through the portals of the schools.

In rural districts, however, and in certain lowly suburbs of towns and cities in the South, the "darky" can still be seen. Enough scraps and bits of cloth are left to give a very fair idea of the kind of goods that once filled the store.

Of course the country negro is nearer the straight goods, and hence the most interesting, but the class of colored people that stand midway between the educated town brother, and the uneducated tiller of the soil, constitutes a study in itself and is brimful of interest.

The semi or partially educated negro, occupying mainly a kind of middle ground, but making in speech and life sudden inroads and excursions, first into one realm and then into the other, keeps the mind in a state of perpetual astonishment, while the general conglomeration at times of all the parts in a single individual before us, makes something so rich and unique that the mind thrills at the possession of what is both social phenomena and psychological treasure.

One feature of the character now alluded to, is a mania for big words. Sometimes the proper one would be aimed at, but through ignorance of the dictionary on the one hand, and a certain readiness of mental furnishing to remedy the defect on the

other, that word would come forth from the lips of
the speaker so strangely beheaded and re-headed,
so betailed and curtailed, that it would have required the gravity of an Anchorite and the face of
Sphinx to have preserved an unmoved or unsmiling
front.

A few weeks spent in the " Big House," as the
family mansion was called, or a few months in
school, were amply sufficient to produce the will-
ingness, if not the ability, to mouth large words
and attempt various elegancies of speech. The
English language was truly a vast and billowy ex-
panse, but the class we speak of never hesitated to
fling themselves upon the waves, and, of course,
would invariably sink. They, however, got used
to drowning. To change the figure, the night was
dark and the country before them broad, uncertain
and unknown, but this did not in the least deter
them, but verbally packing up and folding their
arms as an Arab did his tent, they went forth, and
like one of old, knew not whither they went.

One of this class, of the female variety, returned
to her humble cabin one night quite affected
and inflated with the atmosphere of the palace-like
home where she had been at work. The elegant
demeanor, stately manners and dignified way of

giving orders and directions about the house had profoundly impressed her. She had drunk in the spirit of the mansion, and carried away its lordly airs and doings as one would wear a garment. The robe had not dropped from her even after she entered her own little hovel and was surrounded by her noisy brats who were scampering around on the floor. A majestic wave of the hand which she had brought with her, and a deep-toned command to make less noise had been all unheeded. Whereupon, with elevated chin and appropriate pose of body, she thus delivered herself:

"I'll let yer know when I say *thus and forth*, hit's got to be did! Do yer hyer me?"

They heard her this time, and were brought into immediate silence, whether by the woman's manner or the remarkable expression, "thus and forth," we do not know; only they were subdued.

Another one of this class, while making a fire in the bedroom of his employer early one morning, was expatiating upon a robbery in the neighborhood the night before. While narrating the occurrence, he would alternately stoop to blow the embers into a flame, and then rise to a kneeling position upon the hearth to hear and answer ques-

tions about the absorbing incident from his employer who had not yet arisen.

" Who do they think broke into the house,
Sandy? "

" Dey say, Mars John, hit was midnight magruders."

There was a suspicious snort from the bed, and
then a choking kind of utterance,

" You mean midnight marauders, Sandy."

" Yes, sah, dat's it, midnight magruders," and
Sandy stooped down to blow the fire, unmindful of
the shaking bed, and inwardly delighted over the
possession of a new and imposing colloquial term.

A third individual in this class had been to town
with the market wagon. On his return, his mistress questioned him as to whether he had seen a
certain lady friend of hers, a Mrs. Judge Somebody.

" Oh yessum, I seed de Judge's wife herse'f.
En I tole her dat you was er wishin' ter see her,
en she *eggserved* dat she would like ter see you."

The quivering eyelids, rolling head, unctuous
voice and evident pride with which the sable speaker
delivered himself of the word " eggserved," made
a picture too exquisitely rich and refreshing for
anyone to properly describe by pen, pencil or

brush. The word, "eggserved," however, was promptly captured, framed and hung up in the family gallery, so to speak. Often it was taken down and used in certain domestic junctures and happenings, and always with powerful effect.

Still a fourth instance comes to the mind of the writer.

A lady cousin of the author was expressing to her dining-room servant her sorrow at the tidings of the death of the girl's father. She added:

"I had not heard, Nancy, that he was so ill."

"Yessum, Miss Ma'y, his health was *decaying* some time."

From the expression of the young colored woman's face it was evident that the word, "decaying," had brought her sweet and decided comfort in the midst of her bereavement.

But our cousin continued,

"What did you say was the matter with your father?"

"De doctor say, Ma'am, dat he had de Locomotive Axlegrease."

"The what, Nancy!" gasped our cousin.

"De Locomotive Axlegrease, Ma'am. Yessum, dats what de doctor say."

A gentleman was present in the room at the time,

but from the apoplectic appearance of his face it seemed as if he would not be present anywhere on earth very long. Laboring for self control, he turned to the girl and spoke, while his voice shook as if he had a swamp ague.

" Nancy, you mean Locomotor Ataxia."

" Yes, sah, dats what I mean, Locomotive Axle-grease."

The climax, however, is reached in a fifth case, where one colored brother had been made to feel perfectly outraged by the persistent misbehavior and wrongdoings of another. Full of righteous indignation, he rolled out the following remarkable sentence :

" No, sah : he would neither be provised nor condesuaded, but was always intermined to act recording to his own destruction."

XXVI.

D. D.

"COME hither, my son, and while we rest under this pine, which seems to be whispering the secrets of the forest behind us to the murmuring, inquiring ocean yonder, that leans far over the strand to hear, then retires as if meditating upon what it has heard, then rushes forward again with another moan-like question ; and while the eye takes in the gleaming white lighthouse far up the coast, and yonder distant, motionless sail, and the smoke trail of the passing steamer still farther away towards the horizon, let me ruminate aloud to thee.

"This is the month of June. The season of college commencements is over. Essays, able and scholarly, and bound with pink and blue ribbon, have been read by sapient youths and able girls of sixteen. Questions, problems and mysteries of all kinds in the realms of art and science, poetry and philosophy, morals and religion, have been met, mentally grappled with, solved, cleared up and made generally luminous in the aforesaid essays. The thing is settled now for the world, and for that matter, so is the essay. It may be found after this present month, well settled in the bottom of an old trunk, in some far-away country home, without hope of resurrection.

"Commencement, my son, is over. The speaker invited from a distance has returned to the bosom of his admiring family, who have already read, in the telegraphic column of the newspaper which he forwarded, that his sermon, or address, was able, erudite, polished and eloquent. (The man sending the report or dispatch not having heard it.) And now the returned speaker bears about with him for several days a look of chastened triumph ; but after that period, and after two or three dozen adroit allusions to the marked attention of his audience, the sudden burst of applause, etc., etc., the said speaker quietly subsides into the jog trot experience and ordinary appearance of a commonplace, everyday life that is unrelieved by platform introductions, hand-clappings, assumed mannerisms, studied deportment, dignified bearing, public honors, elaborate dinings, and a general kind of happification.

"Yes, commencement is over ! The red hot college brand, D. D., has been flourished, applied vigorously, and the smell of scorched ministerial flesh is in the air."

" Father, what is D. D. ?"

" What is D. D. ? I came near saying it was not much ; but on reflection I would say it amounts to nothing.   Still to speak more intelligibly, it does not stand for ' Doubly Dead,' as some rashly sup- pose, or ' Dry as Dust,' as others have maliciously suggested. It is one of the many remarkable com- binations of the alphabet whereby some individuals are made glad, others sad, still others mad, while a chartered institution of education is relieved of a heavy burden."

" I hardly understand you, father."

" It is not difficult to comprehend, my son. At one time it was thought that the great and only function of the alphabet was its service as a medium of communication between man and his fellow. This was a very hasty and incorrect conclusion. As men have grown wiser, discoveries have in- creased and inventions of all kinds blessed the earth.   Among them, and prominent at that, is the sublime art of using the alphabet, and especially parts of the alphabet, not to spell, but to throw a spell ; not to reveal, but to hide a meaning ; not to add to mental burdens, but to deliver from bur- dens.   For instance, a body of gentlemen, repre- senting a certain educational institution that is weak in its knees from a number of causes, can by a wise use of one or more letters of the alphabet not only help a friend, make a friend, and advertise a business, but can also pay a debt, all to the comfort and relief of the institution itself."

" But how, father?"

" The whole thing is done by taking two or three letters, arranging them in a certain form, and applying them to the name, and you might say, to the person of some individual, who thereafter becomes the lifelong friend, defender and advertiser of the aforesaid institution. This curious disposal of letters and their application constitutes a college brand.

" The only arrangement difficult for most of these colleges to make is the following, L. S. D., which is supposed to stand for pounds, shillings and pence, or their equivalents. Failing at this point, they make up for it with other combinations. But even here it requires much skill and a nice judgment. It would never do to trust to a chance disposal of letters, for some exceedingly painful pictures and images could be mentally produced by two or three letters infelicitously connected.

" We do not dwell here, but pass on with the statement that in a certain University in England

it had been the custom to require an essay from
each minister who was to be honored with the title
of D. D.   But another law was passed by the faculty, demanding two essays, whereupon the college poet and wit became inspired and gave forth
the following affecting lines to the town paper,
which as promptly published them :

> "The title D. D.
> 'Tis proposed to convey,
> To an A double S
> For a double S A."

" Chance arrangements of letters as suggested
above would never do.   No matter how the public
might believe that the preacher had earned and
deserved the title, yet the feelings of the man himself should be considered.

" Suppose that a college in a fit of absence of
mind should settle on the letters D. H., as we once
saw a hotel clerk do, attaching these very two
characters to the name of a preacher who had
departed without paying his bill.   What, then ?

" We felt that day, as we saw that peculiar
suffix garnishing the clerical name, like saying to
the clerk and owner :

" Sirs, you do this gentleman great wrong ; you
have mistaken a letter. He is not a D.H., but a D.D.

" But no, it seemed that they knew him better than I did, and that hotels had titles, degrees and brands as well as colleges, and they reserved the right to apply certain letters to names as do certain universities. Theirs were P'd and D. H. But all this is a digresssion.

" The colleges do not stop with one brand, they have many. They possess, we may say, a number of kaleidoscopic combinations, which never fail to please.

" It is true that some of their arrangements possess a double meaning or significance, according to the faith or unbelief of the public. For instance, M. D. stands for Doctor of Medicine, but some insist it is the old word, " Murder," with the four smallest letters left out. B. A. is regarded by college circles to mean Bachelor of Arts, and by many of the outside world as representing great knowledge and acquirements, but others gravely affirm that it is a part of the exclamation BAH !, the last letter having been purposely left out.

" So thoughtful, observant men asseverate that S. T. D., stands for 'Stalled !' and Ph. D., is an agreeable, but cunning way of altering the word ' Phooled !'

" The degree LL. D. was originally L. S. D.,

(pounds, shillings and pence), but the middle letter was changed from S. to L. to prevent any reflection upon the profession.

" Nor is this all, my son. As men become great, or college debts and obligations greater, it does not matter which, these and still other titles will be added in such number that it will become a question as to what part of the alphabet will be left to us common mortals ; and further still, what visiting card or envelope will ever be able to contain, in a sense, the individual's greatness.

" For instance, several years ago I received a letter from a preacher, and in it was one of his cards. I repeat it just as it was written, or rather printed, only changing the real name to the fictitious one of Brown, the changed name, by the the way, possessing the exact number of letters that were in the real one. Here it is :

"W. Brown, M. D., D. D., LL. D.

"At a glance the eye takes in the fact that the added letters outnumber the original name by one already, and still the man was alive and increasing in fame.

" The same year we had another visiting card sent us by a ministerial friend, which bore the following legend, the family name only changed, though having the same number of letters. The rest is exactly copied from the card :

"W. H. Long, A. B., M. A., Ph. D., D. C. L., LL. D.

" Now, it is impossible to contemplate these two addresses without being peculiarly affected. One emotion excited is that of sympathy and pity for a man who has to sign such a longitudinal name. Second, a sensation of alarm is aroused as we are made plainly to see that with these increasing signs of greatness no man can hold his patronymic very long on his visiting cards. Just a glance at the addresses of Brown and Long will reveal the approaching peril. Already close to the lefthand border, it is evident that with two or three more degrees the family name, already retiring in the background, will finally be pushed entirely off the envelope or enamelled pasteboard, and nothing be left but a riotous, triumphant portion of the alphabet, spelling nothing, and for that matter, meaning nothing.

" A third feature about the matter which awakens thought and concern in the observant mind is the obvious injustice done the family name by this preponderance of letters on one side of the patronymic, while the other is severely neglected, as for instance in one of the addresses **already** given :

"W. H. Long, A. B., M. A., Ph. D., D. C. L., LL. D.

" Evidently Mr. Long is flying with one wing and should have another. There should be symmetry in names and visiting cards, as well as in the shape of birds and form of houses. A building with a wing attachment on one side must have another to correspond on the opposite quarter, or the eye, taste and judgment of observers will be offended.

" Realizing this, men have gone to work on the lefthand side of the name and added various kinds of balance weights. Not allowed to use letters alone, colleges having a monopoly upon them, they took whole words, as for instance, His Majesty, His Gracious Majesty, His Highness, His Royal Highness, His Excellency, the Honorable, etc., etc., etc.

" The church, not to be outdone, rushes into this struggle to redeem and save the family name, or more truly to prize or lift up the neglected or sinking end of it to a proper level with the righthand attachments, and so we have the titles Reverend, Right Reverend, Most Reverend, His Grace, His Holi-

ness, etc. etc.   Then comes a long array of Bishops, Elders, Deacons, Arch Bishops, Arch Deacons, Rectors, Curates, Canons, Vicars, Deans,
and others too numerous to mention.

" The result is that at last the prefixes are equal
in number to the suffixes, and the family name of
Brown, Long and others can be not only redeemed,
but placed in right relation to all the various borders of card or envelopes by being sandwiched between letters on one side and words on the other.
To illustrate, a certain address I once saw, read as
follows :

" The Right Reverend Thomas Green, D. D.,
Ph. D., LL. D.

" Here we see the good old name of Green is
properly balanced.   If anything, the prefixes, or
lefthanders, have the advantage over the suffixes,
or right-handers, when it comes to an actual enu-
meration of letters.

" The introduction of such a favored gentleman
in a large dining-room, or at a public reception,
would be high sounding, euphonious and ornate to
the highest degree,—' Ladies and gentlemen, allow
me to present to you, His Grace, the Right Reverend Thomas Green, Bishop of Soandso, A. M.,
D. D., Ph. D. and LL. D.'

"Sometimes I have thought, as I have seen the colleges capturing the alphabet by sections, that it would be a good plan for the people to rise en masse and throw the tea overboard, so to speak, or to pass a Declaration of Independence and every man wear the whole alphabet like a kind of necklace about his name as follows:

"a b c d e f g h i j k l mJohn Smith n o p q r s t u v w x y z.

"Perhaps in this way, by standing up for our rights, we might stop in a measure this robbery and ignoring of our rights upon the alphabet, which belongs to us all."

."But, father, what has all this to do with D. D?"

"Everything, my son. D. D. is one of the favorite college brands, and very freely and liberally it is applied. Sometimes it is given medicinally, for it has been known to build up a depleted ministerial system. Cartright, the pioneer preacher, however, rejected it on that ground, saying that he thanked God his divinity did not need doctoring.

"Sometimes it is given gratefully, in recognition of past favors or anticipation of some benefit to be received from the branded."

" Why, father, you surprise me. I thought a person who received this degree had to possess great attainments in theology, with knowledge in science and general literature, that he had to understand Greek and Hebrew, to be a mighty expounder of God's Word, and a man indeed great in head, heart, deed and life?"

"Well, that might have been the case, once, but times have changed, my son, and the world is getting a new theology, or truer still, trying to get along without any at all. And then the preachers are numerous, and some are ambitious, and some clamorous, and above all, colleges are plentiful, especially small colleges, and this latter class has no idea of possessing prerogatives and not exercising them, of owning a brand and not using it."

"Do all the colleges bestow these titles with equal freeness?"

"Oh no. The small surpass the great in this regard. In England the title D. D. is rarely given, and means considerable. In this country our great universities bestow it more frequently than is done across the ocean, but still with some caution. It is the small college which wearies not in this work and that seems possessed with the idea that this is its mission and purpose, to make D. D's."

"I should think that preachers would prefer the title from a large and old institute of learning."

"They do, and so many of them are kept in terror, dodging the honors of one of these smaller places. But it is of no avail. The small college watches the papers and pulpits, and as soon as a man emerges above the line of mediocrity, one of these college Boards, with their President at the head, rush forth upon the rising individual with the college brand all red hot with resolutions, and applying it to him vigorously, mark him forever as their own."

" I judge, father, that some thus served feel annoyed."

" Annoyed ! That is not the word. Some fairly sicken, and others inwardly rage in their mortification. I was told of a certain individual, that he had lived and striven for a great university marking title, and felt the day was drawing near for that consummation, as his articles and discourses began to attract public attention. But one summer, having delivered an able address at the Commencement of a small country college, the Board instantly called a meeting, and with great enthusiasm passed a vote, heated the irons, and rushed with

one accord upon the man and branded him with
their brand.   He gave a great public outcry !   It
was sounexpected? So painful ! Some report that
in his acknowledgment of the Liliputian honor
he said, 'he would rather have received this title
from the hands of Pine Brush College, founded
here in Black Jack Neighborhood, than to have
had it come from the largest and oldest University
in the world,' etc., etc.

''My informant also told me that as the branded
man talked on, he actually foamed at the mouth.

''But the little colleges do not stop to consider
the pain they inflict.   They feel it is their mission
and privilege, and so in the month of June, the
branding season, they dash into the thickest of the
fight, and soon the dull thud of the brand is heard,
the scream of the victim arises, the acknowledg-
ments flow like blood or ascend like wails, according to the fancy of the looker on.   The battle cry
is, brand somebody if you can, but before you
brand nobody, be sure to brand anybody.''

"But at this rate, father, there will soon be no
preachers left without the title."

"Yes, that is true.   We are rapidly approaching
that period when all will have it."

"Well, if that be so, what will the colleges do

in their distribution of these prizes, or I should more respectfully say honors?''

"They can give other titles like Ph. D. and S. T. D., and after that invent new ones."

"But, then, father, there must even be and end of this. And what is more the very commonness and abundance of these degrees will cause their depreciation, and utter inability to impress the public mind."

"Exactly so, my son. And doubtless you think by this turn of the question, this presentation of the inevitable, that you have placed the colleges and myself in a quandary. Not at all. With prophetic gaze I see the deliverance, the way of escape from this great difficulty. For would it not be a difficulty and trouble indeed for a college to lose its branding irons? A college unable to confer degrees or titles would be like a physician unable to get hold of physic or a man powerless to reach his purse. Indeed, more, Othello's occupation would be gone.

" But mark you, this is the way of escape and deliverance. When all that are preachers are D. D.'s ; when prominent personages are loaded with titles, as the hull of a vessel is covered with barnacles, then the College Brand will be given up for a different looking instrument altogether, —something not of a stamping, but extracting power, not a Brand, but a huge pair of Forceps.

"So it shall be that when this or that minister comes up to a College Commencement with the ache and throbbing pain of a D. D. upon him, and suffering from the decayed honor of other titles, and he shall by sermon or address, or by scholarly attainment or noble performance cover himself with glory, the faculty and trustees shall consider his case, diagnose his moral worth and intellectual excellence, and if pleased, shall then and there solemnly bring out the Forceps of the College and with a tremendous jerk forever pull out the dead and hollow D. D. from his name. After that, if he is a man of real merit, and they would do him even greater honor, they will proceed to extract the decayed Ph. D and S. T. D. with their twisted roots, until finally the table is fairly covered with ecclesiastical teeth.

"Oh the relief to the sufferer! With groanings these grinders and incisors were drawn out, for they had gone deep into the ministerial nature and curved around the hidden man, but they were removed at last, and now with tears of joy the relieved man thanks the Board of Professors for their able extraction of roots, and gladly pays any charge the Faculty and Trustees may be pleased to make.

"Verily it shall come to pass in those days, and they are nigh at hand, when it will be to a man's honor that he is without a title, and has no plume-like, or tail-like appendage to his name."

XXVII.

L ET artists and travelers boast as they will about Halls of modern Art and Galleries of ancient paintings, of the Old School and the New School, of the Vandykes and the Rembrants, of the collections of London, Paris, Rome and Florence, yet it remains a fact that living men and women hold us with a stronger spell and a more lasting power than the creations of brush, canvas and colors can possibly exercise.

It is a rare thing for a person to visit a work of art many days and pour over it for hours at each visit. The rule is that one look is sufficient for the greater number of paintings, the study of one hour exhausts others, and few can stand repeated visits. Whatever may be the depth of the finest subject on canvas, yet this fact remains that in itself, it is motionless and doomed to changelessness. It is what the artist made and left. The fancy may invest it with hidden charms, and yet there are the same colors, the old, fixed stare and the unaltering attitude.

Besides all this, some of us are unable to visit these Museums and Halls of Art, and few are able to return after a first visit.

It is fortunate for us that we have the Life Gallery all around us. On the cars, on the street, at home, in our constant contact with people in the paths of business and pleasure, we see full-length, life-size portraits that surpass in their effect, in many respects, the pictures of the Louvre and the Vatican. Our paintings have stepped down and out of all kinds of frames and settings. No canvas or cloth of any character can hold them. They furnish their own color and groupings. We do not have to walk down an endless aisle to see them, but they stream in a procession by us. They have motion. They have a delightful changeability that the ordinary portrait fails to possess.

So we repeat, fond as we are of works of Art, we prefer Nature. We would rather look upon the Gallery of Life, if choice had to be made, than to be confined to the Hall, which is only filled after all with imitations and representations of life.

Many of the individuals we have met in the past, and many of the life scenes beheld, have become themselves paintings, and hung up in the

halls of memory, make a wonderful Picture Gallery. Some of us feel very rich in these posses-
sions, and there are days when we lock ourselves in
these Halls of the Mind and walk silently up and
down the aisles of Recollection and gaze upon
these personages and happenings of the Past.
Sometimes the children or our friends catch us
smiling or sighing as we stand meditatively with
hands folded behind us, looking at one of these old
time portraits. They ask us why we laughed, or why
the tears fell upon the cheek, and we hastily brush
away the drops and say, "Oh, it was nothing."

On certain days when the little ones beg us, or
our friends have ingratiated themselves to an
unusual degree, we take the key and show them
some of these mental treasures. Some we do not
care to let any one look at, such are their precious-
ness and sacredness. When we have attempted to
go down this private aisle, people have wondered
why the eyes have overflowed when standing before
and talking about one of these life pictures. But
we tell them that the dust we brushed off the frame
and canvas got into our eyes and some into the
throat, producing a choking sound which made our
auditors look very hard at us. But it was simply
the dust.

These things have made us avoid taking visitors down what we call the Hidden Gallery, but there are other halls and corridors that are well supplied, and some days we allow the public to come in and take a stroll.

We have opened the door this morning to exhibit a few pictures in one of the outer galleries. Here is one that I call,

"SORROW AND POVERTY."

It was drawn, or rather beheld, at a little railroad station in Kentucky. A plain-looking woman got off the train and was met by a plain-looking man. They were both evidently in middle life and in humble circumstances. They appeared to have had a hard time in this world. But the thing that touched me most was their possession of some unknown, common sorrow; for immediately after meeting they walked off side by side with the tears rolling down their faces. The man with a coarse bandana handkerchief kept wiping his eyes, while the woman's hand was busy in a like employment. What was it? Perhaps she had come from the deathbed of a loved one dear to both. Perhaps she had been summoned to a sick bed here, and had arrived too late, and had been so informed.

We can not tell. But as they walked off, unnoticed by the crowd, two plain, simple people plunged in a common grief, the scene appealed most powerfully to the heart. The unstudied grief, the poverty of the couple, their isolation from everybody, their silent turning away into an empty-looking world with their burden, made the living picture all the more heart moving. They knew it not, but tender sympathy and prayer went up in their behalf from at least one heart that morning on the train.

The next picture I have named,

" A CHILD'S SORROW."

At a small station in Texas I heard two children crying bitterly outside. One especially was loudly lamenting and saying something I could not understand. Looking out of the window, I saw a girl of twelve wrapping her arms around another girl of ten and trying to pull her from the grasp of a man who was drawing her toward the train. Then came the thrilling, pleading, eye-filling words :

" O don't take my sister. O my little sister, I can't let you go. O please don't take her. Don't take my little sister."

Such was the strength that the agony, even

frenzy, of the girl gave her, that the man found
himself unable to separate them, while the conductor had already cried out, "All aboard."

Here a second man sprang forward and both
managed to separate the two weeping girls, and
thrust the younger up the steps into the car. No
one who witnessed the scene will ever forget the
wail of grief and gesture of despair of the older
child when she realized her helplessness and saw
her sister borne away. I heard her cry, "O my
God—my poor little sister!"—and the roll of the
train drowned the rest.

As I gathered the history afterwards, it was a
parting compelled by poverty. A poor woman
with five or six little girls found herself unable to
take care of them all, and one of the youngest was
given to a gentleman in Alabama to adopt, and he
had thus taken her away.

The third I call,

"THE PINEY WOODS."

The scene is that of a great shadowy forest
made up entirely of those lofty-plumed, sad-voiced
trees, belonging to the family of palms and called
the pines. The great trunks shoot up like pillars
to hold a ceiling or canopy of interlocked boughs,

so thick as to fill the woods even at midday with solemn shadows. Long aisles carpeted thickly with yellow needles, and sprinkled with burrs, open in every direction and tempt the musing wanderer to lengthy rambles.

But the ceiling overhead is also a marvelous musical instrument. It is Nature's greatest æolian harp. The sharp, green needles furnish all the notes needed, even to the deepest minor chords. Suddenly a zephyr comes out of the South, and a far away, weird sound is heard, full of melody, like spirit voices high up in the air. You glance upward and see the plumed heads gently stirring and bending, while shaking down this unwritten music upon your soul, It dies away. And then suddenly it rises again with a profounder sigh, a more sorrowful wail, under the spell of which memories are aroused, long vanished forms and faces return, and an unutterable yearning for something and somebody takes possession of the spirit, so that the eyes fill and overflow, and the heart feels as if it would certainly break.

Beautiful, melancholy grove of the South! many a time in early life have we strolled, book or gun in hand, through its shadowy aisles, drink-

ing in its sweet, resinous breath, or stretched on its
clean, brown sward, listened to the plaintive music
in the tree tops. Often at the hour of sunset or twi-
light we have heard from afar the lonely call of
the whippoorwill in its fragrant depths, and later
still from the gallery or bedroom window saw the
moon rise over the dark hills and crown the majestic looking woods with a coronet of liquid silver.

The sight of the heather of Scotland always
deeply affected Walter Scott. So the writer can
never see, smell or hear the pines without the eyes
becoming misty and the heart getting home-sick
for the Southland.

The fourth picture we glance at I call,

"THE ORGAN GRINDER."

There is no other city just like New Orleans,
and because of this uniqueness comes its great
charm. The narrow streets, old French and
Spanish houses, beautiful gardens, tropical looking
flowers, delightful gulf breezes, and the majestic
river flowing by its crescent-shaped side, are some
of the features of the place that make it to be en-
duringly remembered.

One of the peculiar features of New Orleans is
the ubiquitous presence of the organ grinder. He

visits, of course, the noisy business thoroughfares,
but abounds most in the residence portion of the
city. Yonder you see him in the dim perspective
of the street with revolving arm, while a few children and a servant maid constitute his audience.
Here you behold him again, bent almost double
under his heavy musical load, approaching the corner where as he plays he can watch four avenues for
beckoning hands. Again we are admonished of his
presence as we hear the strains of the organ wafted
over the shrubbery and tree tops from a neighboring
street. It is an afternoon hour ; the gentlemen are
down town ; the ladies with book or light sewing
sit in hall or swing in hammock ; the soft sea breeze
is just felt through the latticed gallery ; the faint
distant whir of the street car barely penetrates the
quiet side streets, lined with typical Southern
homes, when suddenly through the sunny, slum-
berous air the strains of a distant organ are heard.
It may be a classic or the slap-dash melody of the
day—it may be Annie Laurie, or the more modern
Annie Rooney ; or it is Marguerite, or Il Trovatore,
and the strains of "Ah, I Have Sighed to Rest Me"
are borne faintly and sweetly to the listening ear.
Whatever it is, somehow we listen ; sensibilities
are stirred, memories revived, and we feel sorry

when the piece is over and the organ grinder gone. A few minutes afterward we hear him again a block further off; a little later the sound is still more faintly heard two blocks distant, and so the melody, like blessings of life, finally dies away altogether.

The fifth is,

"A RIVER SCENE."

When I was a boy I stood one afternoon on the bank of the Alabama River and looked at a steamer going down the stream toward the city of Mobile. The calliope on the upper deck was playing Lorena. As the strains of that pathetic song of the war died, or we might say, faded away in the distance, together with the lessening form of the steamer, I was left spellbound upon the bank. The very ripples of the river seemed as they broke upon the shore at my feet to bring with them fragments of the touching melody that had just ceased reverberating, and out of the distance seemed to come the words of the song:

"A hundred months 'twas flowery May,
  When up the hilly slope we'd climb,
To watch the dying of the day
  And hear the distant church bells chime."

We remember at the time, that the Confederacy

was going to pieces. Federal forces were raiding
the land, and a melancholy not only brooded upon
the people, but seemed to fill the very atmosphere.
Nevertheless there was something in the scene in
itself that left a lifelong impression upon the
writer. It has been a long time since that afternoon, but the swelling of the heart, the indefinable
longings produced by the scene and hour have
never been forgotten.

Some would say, what is there in that simple
circumstance to make a lasting picture ; a distant
bend in the river, a vanishing steamer, the strains
of a love song dying away in faint and still fainter
echoes along the shore, and the river breaking in
a mournful, lapping sound at the feet of a boy?

We reply : some things may never be explained
or described—they can only be felt.

The sixth and last is,

"A CAMP GROUND NIGHT SCENE."

It was a summer night at the Sea Shore Camp
Ground near Biloxi in the "Seventies." From
the tabernacle could be seen the Gulf of Mexico,
or more correctly speaking, the Mississippi Sound,
lying in outspread beauty before the eye and
heaving in gentle billows under the misty light of

myriads of solemn stars. The distant wash of the waves could just be heard as they rolled in upon the beach. A soft, gentle wind came out from the sea and fanned the cheeks of a thousand people who were sitting in the tabernacle. The sermon had just been concluded, and the altar was well filled with penitents, and hundreds of voices were singing in delightful harmony the touching gospel hymn :

> "I need Thee, oh I need Thee,
> Every hour I need Thee,
> O bless me now, my Savior,
> I come to Thee."

Dr. Walker had preached. Dr. Linus Parker, then editor, had briefly exhorted, and now stood in the altar with his eyes fixed on the audience. Bishop Keener, grave and noble of face, sat in the pulpit with that thoughtful, far-away look for which he is distinguished. Preachers by the score were scattered about here and there, singly or in groups, and a solemn spirit or atmosphere rested upon all and over all.

It has been over twenty years since memory took the picture described above, but it is as fresh to-day as then. There was that about the scene and the hour that will not let the colors fade, or the figures pass away.

Many of the people gathered there on that occasion have gone above the stars that shone upon them, and now look face to face upon Him of whom they sang at that service with loving, adoring and wishful hearts. Great also have been the changes among those who still remain of that audience. But the writer never hears the hymn, " I need Thee every hour," but in a moment, the hour, place and people are all back again. Once more the camp-fires are seen twinkling through the trees, he hears the solemn wash of the waves on the strand, he sees the star-lighted sea, the great thoughtful audience, the faces of the preachers, the forms bowed at the altar, while the melody of the hymn surges up again as fresh and tenderly beautiful as when it rolled in harmony over the Camp Ground, and then died away in the shadowy depths of the neighboring forest, on that beautiful summer night in the long ago.

XXVIII.

THE Picture Gallery being somewhat dusty, and thereby affecting the eyes somewhat, as well as the feelings, we take the reader into a side room and show him a few portraits of certain individuals known by the writer in other years.

The five we select out of many are now no longer on earth, but something they possessed remains, and so with loving and faithful hand we have made the pen to act as a kind of pencil or brush and have striven to put on paper as upon the canvas an outline anyhow of men who have variously impressed the writer, and whose lives should not be forgotten.

We commence with Brother N——. He was an itinerant Methodist preacher of fifty years or thereabouts, with iron gray hair, thin, beardless face, a very grave-looking countenance that rarely smiled, but surmounted by a pair of sharp, gray eyes placed close together and which at times fairly sparkled with mirth.

He had such a dry way of saying witty and

cutting things that one would have to look quickly from the quiet-looking face to the twinkling eyes to catch his meaning.

With all this, he was one of the most powerful men in prayer, especially in altar work, that we ever heard. He had a way of reaching climaxes in his public supplications, and as he would make his point, he would bring his hands together with a resounding slap that seemed to drive the nail home and brad it on the other side.

His great ambition was to possess a buggy, that he might travel his circuit with ease and comfort. So after much economizing here and there, he invested.

When the shining, polished vehicle was brought home, he felt at once a burning desire to pay a number of pastoral calls some distance in the country.

The very first night he stopped at a farmer's, where the stable was small, and sheds were none, so that the buggy with its handsome, shining leather trimmings had to be left out in the lane, where at least fifty or sixty cattle were gathered. Brother N—— did not fancy this separation from what was evidently his pride and joy; and that night he dreamed several times that his buggy was stolen.

Next morning he walked out of the house, through the big gate into the lane, and lo! and behold! the cattle and goats together had eaten up every particle of the leather of his buggy, trimmings, flaps, cushion and all, and not a thing was left but the wood and iron, and even some of the wood-work was gone. The spectacle was decidedly spidery to look at, not to say skeleton or ghost-like.

We have heard Bro. N—— describe the occurrence years afterward. Raising his finger and looking around at his breathless auditors, he gravely said.

" Right then and there, brethren,—I fell from grace! "

Blessed man! If he did fall out of grace at that time, he certainly fell in again.

Today he is slumbering in a country church-yard under southern pines that heard his marvelous prayers and burning exhortations in days gone by, and that now sigh and sing in their weird voices about his sleeping head and scatter upon his lowly mound their yellow needles and brown cones as a kind of tribute from nature in recognition of his worth.

The second portrait is that of Brother D——, a

good, simple-minded, old gentleman of sixty-five or seventy years, when he was left a widower.

It was supposed by all up to that time that the Septuagenarian's consuming thought and main preparation in life was for heaven. But after a few weeks it became manifest that Bro. D—— believed the Scripture to the effect that it was not good for man to dwell alone, and that he felt he had a duty to discharge, and that duty was matrimony.

If he had even then chosen a woman in the fifties or even forties, not much would have been said about his second marriage, but he sought for his bride among the youngest of his female acquaintances. It was truly wonderful how he brushed up, pulled a small wisp of gray hair over the big bald spot which covered three-fourths of his head, and tried to look young and spry.

There were many who remembered his unctuous prayers and earnest sermons of other days, and sighed over this transformation which was making the man ridiculous in his old age. But none of these things moved Bro. D——. It is questionable whether he noticed the pity he excited, his infatuation was so great.

At last when he obtained the consent of a young woman to go through life with him, or rather to see him end his, and the happy patriarch had ridden into the county seat for his license, he by the strangest mistake gave to the clerk the name of his son instead of his own.

The blunder was not discovered until next day, when the couple were about to stand up for the celebration of the ceremony. At this juncture it was noticed by the preacher that the certificate had the wrong initials and that Bro. D——'s son and not himself had been duly authorized by the great commonwealth of Mississippi to marry the young woman then on the floor.

Of course this was not to be thought of for a moment, and so all proceedings had to stop until Brother D—— could gallop back to town, fifteen miles away, and rectify the error. As the day was warm, and the whole distance to be traveled thirty miles, and the road was rough, and the rider had been born in the beginning of the century, the task was no little one. And yet it was amusing to see Brother D——'s eager departure, his flapping arms and floating gray hair as he scurried down the road, and pitiful to behold his limp and exhausted appearance when he returned late in the day with his license all right this time, but looking himself as if he was better fit for the hospital than for a marriage feast and ceremony.

Poor old fellow! He only lived a couple of years after his marriage, and was far from happy in those twenty-four months. Somehow the people have forgotten and forgiven that weakness of his old age, and prefer to speak of the really excellent life he lived before the act of folly of his last years. He is without doubt in heaven, where the Great King thoroughly understands how a blundering head can cap and cover a truly good heart.

The third portrait over there is that of Brother F——. one of those young preachers who imagine they are called to the ministry, when everybody else seems to be profoundly impressed that there is a mistake somewhere and that the brother has answered somebody else's call.

The young man we speak of had a frail body, a pallid face, faded blue eyes, sandy hair, and a slow, weak, drawling way of talking. He seemed to lack backbone and that stuff out of which real men are made. He appeared to belong more to the opposite sex than to his own.

He was duly sent to a circuit, but made a complete failure in every respect. His case was taken under consideration and it was decided best for him to go to college a year or so. This he did, and returning to the conference, tried an appointment the second time, when lo ! another failure.

His friends then concluded he needed a course at a theological school and he departed again and spent two years. Once more he returned to the conference to receive a charge for the third time.

A week beforehand he was heard to preach a sermon in which all that the auditor and reporter could remember was that the speaker made a twirling movement of his forefinger in the air and said in his little, thin, die-away voice that " the binary system seems to prevail in the astronomical heavens ; all the stars nearly are double." This was evidently the condensed result of his arduous college labors.

Two weeks later he received with the rest of the preachers his appointment. There was a prompt, expeditious scattering of the brethren, on horseback, in buggy and on railroad train to their charges, whether new or old, near or remote.

A snow storm had come up suddenly the day before, and this was followed by "a freeze." The writer was on his horse galloping down the white and frozen street to reach his first appoitment, ten miles away in the country, when he passed on the corner Mrs. F——, the mother of Brother F——.

The writer stopped a moment to salute her, and ask if her son had gone to his work. Her reply, in a drawling, whining, die-away voice like her son's, was:

"No, Lucien slipped on the frozen snow, and sat down so hard that it has jarred him quite badly, so he went to bed."

"Did he get up this morning?" we soothingly inquired.

"No indeed, he is still in bed. It does hurt Lucien so bad, you know, to sit down sudden on anything that is hard."

"Poor fellow," we said, while our ribs fairly ached with the effort to keep a set of mutinous laughs imprisoned. Tears, however filled our eyes, and the voice choked up so that we very much fear that Mrs. F—— thought she had deeply moved us by her relation of her son's indisposition. And so she had, but not in the way she imagined.

This, we think, ended Brother F——'s call to and work in the ministry. That last jar jolted the idea clear out of his blessed little head that he could "endure hardness" as a good soldier of Christ. Our impression is that he died five years after this from a case of measles that he ought to have had when he was a child.

We are sure that he went to heaven. He did not have energy and force enough to be outbreakingly bad, even if he had preferred to enter upon such a career, The Atonement is so arranged as to provide for the salvation of all the children, and several other classes besides, that we have not time to mention, so we feel certain that he was saved.

We approach the fourth portrait.

Brother M—— was one of the most dignified men we ever met in the ministry. It is true that he did not possess gifts, nor had he performed achievements to give him the right to assume such an impressive and majestic air, but the demeanor was not taken up by reason of these things, but because it was partly natural and mainly preferred. Some men sought knowledge, others cultivated various gifts, but Bro. M—— developed dignity.

If he had been an undertaker, he would have made his fortune. If he had lived in Oriental countries, he would have been a model for the Sphinx, and made Job's friends feel small indeed in being able to keep silent and look solemn for only a few days. Bro. M—— said nothing and looked dignified all the time ! It almost made one tired for him. The ordinary individual could not but feel that it was bound to be exhausting to keep the body unbent, and the facial muscles in such straight lines all the time.

The children stood in awe of him, and young people thought he looked so grave and solemn because he knew so much. One, from his appearance, would have supposedthat when he was not thinking of the Bible, he was brooding on Fox's Book of Martyrs, Hervey's Meditation Among the Tombs, while his lightest thoughts, if allowed to run at all in secular channels, would be Plutarch's Lives and Rollins' Ancient History.

This, we say, was his appearance. The reality was that Bro. M—— had never read any of these uninspired volumes, and often when apparently absorbed in thought, was really thinking about nothing in particular. He had learned what seemed to be the real lesson of life to him,—how to look dignified, and now there was little else to do except to keep dignified and let Time roll on and the Judgment Day come.

One day he was in a country church sitting on a bench that was pinned by large wooden pegs to the wall in the back of the pulpit. Bro. S——, a fiery, demonstrative character, was preaching. Bro. M—— did not preach often, and then mainly delivered what are called, " Funeral Sermons."

He was sent for, far and wide to preach such discourses over deceased grown people and children,
and who had been dead from one week up to twenty
years.

On this occasion Bro. M—— was not preaching, but listening to Bro. S——, the fervent-shout-
ing, hand-clapping and stormy preacher of the
community. Suddenly, as Bro. S—— gave a
spring in the air and came down again with a great
jar on the floor, not only the pulpit, but the whole
floor of the log meeting house came down with a
crash and fell with the entire congregation six or
seven feet. Bro. M—— was sitting on the bench
pinned to the wall, and that being the only seat
which fell not, our grave and solemn-faced brother
was left nine or ten feet up in midair with his back
to the wall and his feet in space. It was a distance
too great for him to leap, and beside, he was too
dignified to even think of such a thing, much less
do it.

Not a soul had been hurt by the accident. And
now as the congregation, glad over its own escape,
looked up and saw Bro. M—— sitting, so to
speak, in midair like a judge, and appearing more
dignified than ever, there was a perfect roar of
laughter.

The bench was narrow and the situation was quite unenviable. The brother refused to cast himself down from the pinnacle, and the hands of the brethren were not sufficiently near his body for him to risk himself and trust to their obtaining a secure hold upon him as he would slip off his perch. Moreover, he did not care to descend that way.

At last some one brought in a plank twelve inches wide and fifteen feet long. The upper end was placed on the bench where the exiled brother was living, and the lower end set against the timbers beneath. Bro. M—— was then advised to slide down, which he proceeded to do with unabated solemnity of manner. As he came slipping rapidly down, the ungracefulness of the body, coupled with the attempted dignity of the face and demeanor, made such a remarkable contrast, that a number of men had to retire and roll on the grass outside with irrepressible mirth, and some in the building buried their faces in their handkerchiefs, appearing to be pictures of grief externally, but it was not the sound of weeping that was heard.

And yet Bro. M—— was a good man and was beloved by many. He died years afterward at peace with God, and in charity with men. He was buried by a Fraternity, with a brass band ahead of the hearse playing a solemn dead march. The measured, melancholy stroke of the town clock can just be heard in the distance by one standing by the tomb of the departed one in the old village graveyard. We cannot but think that this is just as he would have had it, if he had stated his wishes before death. Peace to his ashes.

We stand now in front of the fifth portrait.

Bro. H——— was a simple, backwoods exhorter or local preacher. He was tall, gaunt, beardless, with peaked nose and chin, and with thin, gray hair, having a tendency to curl under at the ends. He was illiterate, had never been to school, and could not speak two sentences in succession correctly, but he was filled with the Holy Ghost. He had a most child-like face, and it was so sunny and smiling and spiritual that one forgot the homely countenance in the beautiful light that shone upon it, and cared not to criticise the ungrammatical speech because of the lovely, holy spirit of the man himself.

Bro. H——— loved a camp meeting above all things, and fairly doted on preaching. It mattered little to him who preached, so Christ was talked about and held up, and it was simply delightful to the observer to notice how the man enjoyed the sermon from start to finish. He kept up a low chuckle of enjoyment, with occasional " bless Gods !" and " glory to Gods," and now and then the old red silk handkerchief would be raised to wipe away the tears that had fallen upon his wrinkled cheeks in response to some peculiarly pathetic presentation of the Cross.

Next to the sermon he valued the Experience or Testimony meeting. The writer well remembers the way he described his conversion. He spoke of his sinful life, of living without God and without hope, and how one day while in his little cornfield the limb of a tree fell upon him.

" It killed me dead," he said in all earnestness and honesty. Whether he failed to distinguish between unconsciousness and death itself, or whether he attributed his recovery to the power of God and his life as a second gift to him, we never asked. But we remember that he said,

" As the folks was packin' me to the house, I hyer'd the bars drap."

He insisted that God had to knock conviction and sense into him with the limb of that tree. His salvation came to him almost simultaneously with his recovery from unconsciousness.

In one of the morning Testimony meetings at which Bro. H—— was present and drawing his usual enjoyment from all the songs and speeches, a pastor of one of our large city churches stood up to give his experience. He said that he had been a great sinner in his day, but God had mercy on him and converted him.

"Bless God!" said Bro. H—— from his seat.

"But after this, I regret to say," continued the preacher, "I backslided."

Bro. H—— sighed audibly and shook his head in a most sorrowful manner from side to side.

"But," resumed the city pastor, "I was graciously reclaimed several years after in a protracted meeting."

"Amen—Thank God!" cried out Bro. H——, who was bending forward in breathless interest.

"It is mortifying" said the preacher, "to have to confess that I backslided again after this."

Bro. H—— here groaned deeply.

"But I thank God," went on the brother from the city, "that I got back again."

"Well," cried out Bro. H—— with his face lifted up full of deep concern, "I hope you stuck that time."

The burst of laughter that followed this sally is

one of the unfading memories of that camp ground.

Bro. H—— through poverty, could not always command the money to pay his railroad fare to this annual meeting, and so one year a minister carried him in his buggy a couple of hundred miles through southern Mississippi to the place. He said afterwards a more devout man he never was thrown with in his life : that he was as unaffected as a child, and his spiritual life was as fresh and fragrant as the beautiful pine forests through which they drove to reach the sea shore.

Every half hour or so this simple-minded lover of the Lord would say,

"Brother L——, please sir, lemme outen the buggy a minute to have er little secret pra'r with the Lord."

Bro. L—— in response would turn the wheel of the vehicle, and Bro. H—— would dive into a thicket, or get behind some great pine trees twenty yards or more away, and then religious services would open. Bro. H——'s "secret pra'r" could be heard several hundred yards away.

In a few minutes this love-sick servant of God would come tramping back through the underbrush with his face all aglow and looking marvelously refreshed. This was kept up during the entire trip of five days.

Moreover, if Bro. H—— stopped at a farm house to ask for a drink of water, after giving the gourd or dipper back to the person who had handed him the drink, he would say to the individual, whether man or woman, and always so humbly and lovingly that they were never offended,

"And now, brother (or sister), let us kneel down and have a little pra'r with the Lord." And down they would all go together on their knees on the gallery.

Just after one of those regular and frequent requests of Bro. H—— to have a little secret prayer in the woods, and had returned chuckling with joy and his face beaming, Bro. L—— turned to him and said,

"Bro. H——, if God was not the most long-suffering being in the universe, you would run Him distracted, for you are always after Him."

In due time, allowing for all Bro. H——'s stops on the way, the two preachers reached the Camp Ground. Services had been going on two days already, but Bro. L—— announced in the Testimony meeting that he had not lost anything, but was really ahead of the crowd before him, for he had been in a camp meeting for five days, held in a buggy, and led by Bro. H——.

The saintly man has been asleep in the piney woods of Mississippi for a quarter of a century. It is very sweet to think that he who sought so diligently to get near and still nearer to the Crucified has been all these years basking and rejoicing in the actual presence of the Redeemer whom he loved so well.

XXIX.

OLD JACK.

THERE are many ways of making a living in this world, and it is fortunate, doubtless, that it is so. We have been made to wonder many times as we stumbled upon methods and ways of keeping soul and body together, and that had been dignified by the name of business. Time would fail to enumerate the small callings and employments that flourish on street corners, back alleys, remote rooms, damp cellars and lofty garrets.

Among the perambulating professions and trades of the street is that of the Dog Catcher. The business of this interesting individual in a large city is to capture during certain seasons of the year all stray dogs that are collarless and unlicensed. The arrest is effected by a piece of wire with a running noose flung skillfully over the head of the unfortunate animal, and then the struggling, yelping, howling victim is first choked into silence and then flung through a kind of a trap door into a cage fastened to the body of a light wheeled wagon. The captors then spring upon the driver's box, crack their whip and drive rapidly away down the street, pursued by yells, cries, groan sand sometimes oaths of grown people, and almost invariably by the screams, wails and lamentations of children to whom the dog belonged or was well and favorably known.

The Dog Pound is generally several miles away on the edge of the city. Here the captive is kept three days, awaiting the redemption of his owner. During these three days, just as men condemned to death are fed bountifully before execution, so these confined animals have a like kindness extended to them. On the third day, however, if no one appears to claim and pay the fine and license, the doomed creature is put to death.

It is a notable sight to see the collection of good and bad looking dogs gathered in this place. Every breed is represented in these rooms of confinement ; curs, spaniels, setters, terriers, with now and then a mastiff or a noble looking Newfoundland. Some of them are evidently pets and highly cared for, but others have a neglected, woe-begone appearance and bear the marks and bearings of dogs who pick up a scant living in back alleys and spend their lives in avoiding flying brickbats and scalding water.

While a bounty, so to speak, is on the heads of all canines in the summer months, yet the Dog Catcher prefers the capture of the yard and household pets for reasons too apparent to mention. Not allowed by law to invade the premises for his prey, he is permitted on the other hand to swoop down upon and fling into his wagon cage any dog he finds on the street without a collar, no matter how handsome, dignified and valuable such an animal may be.

Hence to carry on his business successfully, the Dog Catcher does not herald his approach with clarion notes like the "Charcoal Man," or with the ringing bell of the "Scissors Grinder," but driving up rapidly to a corner, his two assistants leap from the wagon, and in a single minute's time the meditative cur in the middle of the street, and the gazing house dog just outside the protecting yard gate on the pavement find themselves suddenly lassoed, and in far less time than it takes to tell it, their terrified howls are throttled, and choking and struggling in stalwart hands they are lifted from their feet and flung into the cage. In another instant the lassoers leap upon the wagon, the driver gives the fleet horse a sharp blow, and away they disappear down the street in a cloud of dust amid the shrieks and cries of children, loud disapproving tones of men, and vociferous explanations of the suddenly assembled street crowd to questions put from opening doors and windows and passing pedestrians. A few minutes more and the groups scatter, men pursue their way, and all that is left of the excitement are conversations held in neighboring houses about it, and the bitter weeping of children whose Rover or Fido has been taken away from them, sometimes for a day, and oftentimes forever.

Thus it is evident to the reader that of all callings there are few more detested and condemned than that of the Dog Catcher. The children regard him as their born enemy, and even many grown folks can not bear him. So when in some early morning hour a sudden yelping and howling on the street is quickly followed by a choking, strangling cry, like an electric flash the whole thing is understood by the neighborhood, and the cry " Dog Catcher ! " arises from every lip and is heard in every tone of pain and disgust. Then follows an uproar on the street, loud cries of protest, some brutal laughs, wails and weeping, a rattle of retiring wheels, and then all is over. Repeatedly we have seen our breakfast table circle of eight completely disappear from the dining room by that single thrilling cry on the street, "Dog Catcher!"

Somebody, we suppose, must be Dog Catchers, as there must also be a hangman, but he who has witnessed a single scene of this kind, caught a glimpse of the choking dogs, heard the sobbing and shrieking children, beheld the troubled faces of women at the windows, and angry looking countenances of men on the pavement, would certainly never turn to such an occupation from its popularity or any delight that could be in such a mode of making a living.

Hence it is that a mishap or misfortune of any kind to a Dog Catcher is always received with hearty laughs, and cordial smiles of approval by many. Even more, there have been cases where men would not willingly consent to the departure of the old household friend, and so fisticuffs would follow, of so fervent and forcible a nature that the Dog Catcher and his helpers would be glad to beat a retreat.

Only a few blocks from our home, a couple of indignant citizens had pitched into the two lassoers of their dogs in so hearty a fashion that the driver had to come to their assistance. Meantime, while they were all engaged in a face-mauling and nose-swelling struggle, another citizen slipped up to the wagon, opened the cage door, and such another scampering out and scattering away of animals was never seen before since the Ark landed on Mt. Ararat. The dogs came out so rapidly that it actually looked like one long dog of thirty or forty feet in length. This moving line instantly broke up, however, into living sections of individual curs, spaniels, setters and terriers, all heading in different directions. The Dog Catchers promptly left their human antagonists to take after the dogs, but the earth seemed in a friendly and mysterious way to open up for the flying animals, while equally sympathetic store doors did the same, and the whole street was in a broad grin as well as a hilarious guffaw over the discomfiture of the canine captors.

The first time I ever heard the cry and uproar on the street declaring what was happening, I had just time to catch through the window a vanishing glimpse of the flying wagon with three men on the seat applying the lash to the horse, while a group of people, some red-faced and excited, were shaking their heads and talking in loud tones about the occurrence.

Another morning I was more expeditious in

hearing the yelp, howl, curse, and cry. " Dog Catcher ! " mingled with screams of children on the street. I sprang to the window and saw two men with the wire lassoes drawing two struggling dogs into a standing position, before lifting and hurling them into the wagon. One was a snow white setter and the other a beautiful black spaniel, the last being the property of the family next door, and one whose faithfulness as a watch dog I had observed. In a moment's time the wire loop was loosened, and the white setter was lifted up and disappeared like a flash through the trap door. In another instant the spaniel with a pitiful cry also vanished in the cage. In a third second the three men were on the seat applying the whip to the horse, and in a trice the wagon swept out of sight around a distant corner.

It would be hard to describe the sensations of mind and heart just after one of these scenes. The helplessness of the animal, its friendlessness, the refusal or neglect in the vast majority of instances on the part of families to redeem the captured dogs, the vision of the animals' coming death on the third day, all this, with the appearance of anxious, troubled faces on the street and crying children in the yard, necessarily makes a deep impression.

On the morning just referred to we sent over promptly to the neighbor and informed her of the fate of her spaniel, and received the sickening reply that she knew it and did not care, that she was tired of the dog.

We recalled that a number of times we had seen the family go out to parks in the day and amusement halls at night, and leave the dog on guard. And faithfully he discharged his duty. For hours at a time we had seen him refuse to stir from his post of watchful defense, no matter what was transpiring on the street. And when the family returned he always seemed so glad. And yet they said they were tired of him, and so signed the sentence of his death.

Meanwhile we did a little ciphering on a strange kind of problem, in which we added some valuable figures to brute life, and substracted others from certain persons we knew, called human beings; and so as the calculation proceeded, the dog seemed to get the advantage.

All this talk about the Dog Catcher is preparatory to the following occurrence.

*   *   *   *

Old Jack, a large and dignified looking dog, with a white body and several large brown spots, made his first appearance in our yard very much as if he had dropped from the clouds. He was not seen to enter the front or back gate, but was first noticed standing amid the playing children, regarding their frolics with a kind and patronizing air.

The little ones were only too delighted to receive him as a kind of heavenly gift, and so in a few days a very great attachment sprang up between the younger members of the family and the grave looking canine.

He was soon found to be a thoroughly trained dog, though evidently now in a superannuated condition. His obedience was perfect, and his fondness of and gentleness to the children unchangeable. How they rolled and tumbled over him, while our little boy occasionally bestrode the broad, strong back of the big fellow, who walked off with him without the least inconvenience.

To the great grief of the little ones, one morning two boys put in an appearance and filed an energetic property claim upon "Old Jack," as he was now called. Their sorrow as the dog was being led away brought out a gentleman of the household, who found out in a few moments' conversation with the lads that they were perfectly willing to part with Jack for a moneyed consideration. They were begged to state the amount at which they held him, and for which they would dispose of him, and the figure was so small that the writer has no idea of mentioning it here lest it seem to reflect upon the worth and attainments of Jack. The price was paid down to them in the presence of witnesses, and the two young merchants gave a verbal quitclaim to Jack, his person, accomplishments, increasing years, approaching decrepitude and all, forever.

After this Jack became quite a privileged character, coming in and out as he pleased, and preferring always to be admitted at the front door. We are quite sure that he enjoyed the door being opened to him by a servant, as if he was on the best social and visiting plane with the family. He became quite an ornament to the house as he stretched his great white and brown body on the marble steps at the front door, and there slumbered for hours in the sunshine.

One of his recreations was to leave the house a half hour before breakfast, proceed down Washington Avenue for a block, turn up toward Lucas Avenue, and be gone just about thirty minutes, returning promptly in time for the morning meal. This regular visit inspired considerable curiosity in our minds, but we had such confidence in Jack's character and habits that we never insulted him by putting a detective watch on him. We rather suspected, however, that he had an acquaintance in the neighborhood, a purely Platonic affection, however, for the dog's honest look on his return showed that wherever he had been, he had conducted himself like a gentleman.

Another occupation of Jack was to watch the children play in the grassy side yard, or walk sedately, but observantly up and down the pavement in front of the house, as they flashed past him with merry shouts on bicycles, velocipedes and wagons, finally concluding the evening sports with a game of " I Spy " while the electric lights flickered upon them through the rustling leaves of the shade trees that lined both sides of the street of our block.

Old Jack wonderfully enjoyed it all, and gave the whole laughing, romping scene his unqualified approval, though always in a dignified and superior way. Sometimes he would become so interested that he would stand up and gaze after them. Numbers of times he would run with them, but usually he would lie on the broad step of the front door, with his head resting on his fore paws, while his eyes rested watchfully and unweariedly upon the children. Several times I am sure that I caught him smiling. But I may be mistaken here, for Jack was a very grave dog.

Strange to say, with all this family attachment to the gentle and faithful animal, his license had never been attended to and the consequent dog collar attached.

One morning while the family were rising from bed and preparing their toilets for breakfast, a great commotion was heard in the street, the howls, yelps, and choking of dogs, the confused murmur of voices, and the old cry :

" Dog Catcher ! "

Instantly some one of the household ran to the window in time to see a beautiful spaniel hurled into the iron cage. Then suddenly remembering Jack and his habit of taking that early morning stroll, she flew to another window to behold faithful Old Jack in the clutches of one of the Dog Catchers, who was dragging him with difficulty to the wagon, on account of the great size of the dog. He had been captured just outside the gate.

The children, now attracted to the window, at the sight of this harrowing spectacle set up cries, shrieks and lamentations most pitiful to hear. A member of the family ran down to the side yard gate to head off the Dog Catcher and pay the fine, on the spot, and so redeem Jack, but the gate was padlocked and she could not make herself heard or seen on account of the high plank fence. Hastening to the front gate, she reached it just in time to see poor Old Jack flung by two powerful men into the cage, hear the door slam, and behold the wagon drive off with a rush and whir.

There was little breakfast eaten that morning by the home circle, while sorrow, indignation, tears, excited remarks and solemn invocations upon the heads of all Dog Catchers abounded.

We never knew how many friends Jack had in the neighborhood until the news of his capture was flashed by servant and children telegraph lines into the various homes round about. Messages and offers of assistance soon arrived, the door bell was rung repeatedly, and a number of callers dropped in to ask about the matter.

Of course the family lost no time in recovering Jack. A gentleman friend offered his buggy, and person as well, and late in the afternoon dashed out several miles to the Dog Pound.

He found Jack walking around sedately among

his doomed and less fortunate companions, as though no disrespect had ever been shown him, and death was not only a few hours off if he was not claimed and redeemed. He had seen our friend before, and appeared to recognize him instantly, with a look which seemed to say, "I thought you would come for me."

At the gentleman's invitation Jack clambered in his grave way into the buggy, and as there was no room in front, took his position on one of the two seats of the vehicle. Being a well-trained dog, he did this easily and naturally, but sitting erect as he did, his great size brought his head fully a foot higher than that of the gentleman who drove the buggy at his side.

It made such a social equality spectacle, and Old Jack looked so dignified through it all, that as they sped along, down through streets, avenues and boulevards, there was a ripple of smiles and waves of laughter on either side that made one think of the wake that follows a passing vessel.

And so this was the way they drove through the city to the anxious, expectant household. The gentleman had a kind, but somewhat embarrassed facial expression, while Jack adhered to his usual grave appearance, with a slightly confused look hard to describe, but which, mindful of his past record, his weight of years, and his elevated position in the buggy, he kept well under.

What a welcome he received when the buggy was first sighted up the street and swept with a clatter up to the door. It was an ovation! The children had been watching for him from the gate and upper windows for two hours. So with the cry, "Yonder he comes!" the whole house most directly concerned and other houses nearby were emptied on the street. Everybody wanted to help Jack out. The grown people all patted him, while the children hugged him and called him by every pet name in the calendar of love.

While the hour was late and the electric lights had been tessellating the street and pavement with flickering shadows for an hour, yet the children were granted permission to take a few runs with Jack up and down the pavement, and their merry cries and Jack's occasional deep bark of satisfaction put a warm, tender feeling in the hearts of all the grown folks, who were standing on the steps or leaning against the gate, and beholding with smiling faces and yet moistened eyes the happy scene.

It was well for the Dog Catcher that he was not there. Not that anyone would have offered him

personal violence, but he could not have survived
the sight of the happiness of that hour. Then the
popularity of Jack, the rising stock of the dog, and
the constantly sinking value of his own employment in the estimation of everybody around,
would have been more than he could have
endured.

As for the family, which had passed through
such a history that day, they lost no time in secur-
ing a license next day and the attendant collar for
Jack's neck.

As for Jack, good, faithful old fellow, general
inspector, patronizer and sharer of the children's
sports, he seemed pleased with his throat ornament
and walked the pavements, crossed the streets and
paid his morning calls around the corner seemingly
without a thrill of fear. The collar stood for a
license, and the license represented the protection
of a great government. So that all the armies and
navies of the United States were really back of
Jack as he walked around, and all were pledged
to shield his person, and guard his life, so long as
like other American citizens he behaved himself.
Thus escorted, so to speak, and thus wonderfully
defended, Jack was free to go down the evening
slope of life in full pursuit of knowledge, pleasure

and happiness, his bed and board costing him
nothing at our house.

I do not know that Jack knew of this license,
but the family did, and it made us in a measure
sublimely indifferent to the presence and even being
of a Dog Catcher. Sometimes we had suspicions
that Jack had an inkling of what had taken place
for his security, for he certainly looked bolder and
paid no attention whatever to suspicious looking
wagons rattling noisily by. We must confess,
however, that if he did know these things he
never said anything about the matter, Still it is
to be remembered that dogs know a great deal
more than they tell to people.

As for the Dog Catcher, canine destroyer, household pet stealer, and children heart breaker, what
shall we say, but that all the little ones we have
talked to on the subject believe there is no hope
for his salvation so long as he holds to such an
occupation. Quite a number are convinced that
already he is beyond the pale of mercy, and no
matter whether he stops or continues his business,
he can never be saved. Concerning these moral,
psychological and eschatological features of the
case we can not speak at this time. Perhaps it is well
for the Dog Catcher that I should not speak at this

very moment, for I have just returned from the window, where I beheld our little ones and Jack rolling on the grass together, engaged in one of their fascinating romps, with happy laughs and good natured barks indescribably intermingled, and not a solitary care resting upon a single heart of the deeply absorbed group.

*   *   *   *

Three years have passed since we penned the lines above. Faithful, dignified old Jack, after increasing feebleness, fell asleep one night in the cellar to awake no more. He went down to his grave full of years and honor, regretted by a large number of acquaintances and friends and deeply lamented by the family circle of which he had come to regard himself as a member.

We doubt not that certain members of that family most heartily wish that Wesley's idea of the Resurrection of animals may be true, and we know there are one or two of that household that no matter what may be the beauty and attraction of the New Jerusalem, would love to take the children, and accompanied by Jack, have a long, sweet stroll over the green fields of Eden together.

XXX.

POOR LITTLE TOBY.

THE study of character is one of the most fascinating of occupations. Human life in every
social and moral plane is full of interest. In a
sense, people are text-books, and some of them
hold us to the living page with the charm and
interest of a novel. Such people are types. They
have a strongly marked individuality, the possession of gifts and attributes, styles of speech and
mannerisms which differentiate them from all
others.

These interesting, living subjects are found not
simply in high, but in low places. They are met
with on the throne and in the stable; in rural
regions and on crowded city thoroughfares; on
dusty highways under the light of the stars, and
walking on velvet and Brussels carpets with the soft
luster of costly chandeliers falling upon them.
Whenever and wherever found, they are types.
They are refreshingly distinct and different from
other people, have a way of talking and act-
ing in a manner peculiarly their own, and hold

you with the charm of freshness, novelty, or origi-
nality, which makes them what they are. They
may be more or less richly endowed mentally, but
the peculiar power of uniqueness is there.

Dickens found many of his characters on the
streets of London, while Craddock obtained hers
in the mountains of Tennessee. They are to be
met everywhere, and are certain to be recognized
by the thoughtful eye.

The old-time Southern plantations were far more
prolific in the production of interesting personages
and striking characters than many people would
imagine. Two of these claim the reader's attention in this sketch : a mother and her son.

Matilda, or Tildy, as the negroes called her,
was a raw-boned woman of forty years of age.
She had a face as black as the ace of spades, and
possessed a temper that at times was several shades
blacker. She had been married, and in the few
years of wedded life had led her husband a perfect
dance, until one day he contracted some swamp
chills, which shook him out of his body and far
away from the shakings that Matilda used to give
him. He left her two girls, a boy named Toby, and
some old rags in the shape of his worn-out clothing.
The sable-colored widow philosophically took the

better portion of the garments and transferred them into her quilts, while one or two pair of trousers descended to Toby, and for that matter, descended far below him, as he was only three feet high, while his father was, or had been a six-footer. After the husband died, Matilda worked off her spasms of fury upon her children. She had a way of paying her respects to them with broom-sticks, hoe-handles and brickbats. Being a woman of ungovernable temper, when she started to punish them, she would use the first thing available as an instrument of correction. A wooden handspike, pair of tongs, or an iron poker were eminently satisfactory to her when she was on the warpath.

In the course of time the girls were placed elsewhere in some kind of farm or housework, and Toby was left to receive the undivided attentions of his mother in the way we have just mentioned.

The child was eight years old when the mother was brought from the quarters and installed as one of the house servants. From this time, my attention was attracted to the peculiar way the mother had of bringing the boy up, or rather knocking him down. He was a black-faced, kinky-headed child, with a curious look, compounded of suspicion, fear, and pleading. If he ever possessed a hat I never knew it; he went bare-headed as well as bare-footed for four years of his life, to my certain knowledge. He was arrayed some days in a coarse, Lowells shirt which descended midway between his thighs and knees; and on other days, in a pair of trousers which had belonged to his father. Matilda cut off about twelve inches from the legs, and gathered in the garment at the waist, with a great rudder-like bulge behind, but still they were too large in every way, and were rolled up at the bottom in liberal folds, while the waistband was so loose that Toby had to hold the garment up with his left hand when standing or walking, to keep it from leaving him altogether. When sitting or lying down, he had some relief from his task of pantaloon support, but the instant he rose to a perpendicular position, the danger of being suddenly denuded stared him in the face, and he would immediately resume the old hand-hitch on the waistband.

He never appeared wearing both these gar-ments, the shirt and trousers, at the same time. This would have been rolling in luxury, indeed! The shirt days were the happier, if the boy could be said to have any happiness at all. On these occasions, he had nothing to hold up with his hands or to encumber him in one of his precipitate flights from his mother. The shirt was not only more agreeable to Toby in a general way, but, in the sudden maternal sallies, it proved to be a special blessing in giving greater freedom to the little black legs in the way of escape. At such times, the end of the garment stood out on a line with the horizon, and no kettle drum sticks ever came down with greater rapidity than did his feet strike the surface of the earth. But the day he wore the pants was not only one of physical discomfort, but positive terror to him; for all retreats were executed with fears of tripping, and falling into the hands of his pursuer.

Sitting in the house one day I heard something strike the side of the building with a resounding bang. Going quickly to the door, I had a glimpse of Toby vanishing at full speed in the distance, with the angry mother at his heels. The battle that morning had opened with a brick thrown at the boy, but which had fortunately missed him and hit the house. If it had struck him, there would have been an immediate end of the lad.

Often after this, I have heard a commotion in the yard and, on hastily going out, would see one of those suddenly instituted pursuits. The child, nimble of foot, and expert at dodging from long practice, could be seen fairly flying, keeping out of the way of rocks, chunks of wood and flat irons, and finally, through the intricacies of the back yard and outhouses, disappearing in the remoter depths of the garden or orchard.

If some one should ask why such conduct was tolerated by a humane and well-regulated Southern home, the answer is that Matilda was not only a first-class washer and ironer, but quick to do anything in the shape of work. She was as smart as she was high-tempered. In addition, she had a most indulgent mistress, who did not like to worry herself much about anything. When one of these sudden bangs against wall or fence would resound through the house, and there would follow the sudden uproar of voices and laughter which always followed this outbreak of war, with flight and pursuit, Mrs Carleton would ask one of the servants.

"What on earth is the matter out doors?" and the servant, with shining rows of teeth, would say.

" 'Tain' nuffin' 'tall, Miss Ma'y, 'cep'n Tildy arter Toby." And so the matter would drop.

Two surprising things were connected with these storms. One was, that the offence of the child was often of the most trifling nature, the dropping of a tin cup, or the failure to hear his mother speak, etc. Then the chase began, with interested observers popping their heads out of kitchen windows and cabin doors, broad grins steadily enlarging on black and yellow faces, while the bang of a rock against the fence, narrowly missing the fugitive, would bring forth a stentorian guffaw from the men and shrill laughter from the women. As the dress of negro children is generally arranged with a view to ventilation, and Toby was specially favored in this regard, the sight of the bare-legged, bare-footed racer with his slim, black limbs twinkling over the ground, and his old shirt standing on end as he fled, brought loud shouts of amusement to the colored observers, although the whole affair was anything but amusing to Toby. He was always terribly in earnest and had to be, as he ducked and dodged from missiles ranging from one to five pounds in weight, any one of which could easily have killed him.

Matilda's language to Toby was pretty much after the same pattern as her bodily treatment of the child, the tongue being as severe as the hand. It was :

" Come hyer ter me, you triflin' whelp?" or

" I'll break ev'y bone in yoh body wid dis flat iron, you black monkey, you !" or

" I'll bust yoh haid wide open wid dis stick !" etc., etc.

There were other expressions with which Toby was often favored when the maternal thermometer ran high, that we do not care to repeat.

To pass the door of the lowly cabin in which the family lived, was to notice that a kind of rattling musketry fire of scolding was the general order of things, varied now and then with a fortyfour pounder explosion. It only required a few minutes pause outside the door for the ear to note the orbit daily described by the woman's tongue. First there was a muttering, a kind of low, fussing tone, then a sharp cry to one of the children.

" Git out o' dat !"

" Whut you doin' thar ?"

" Come hyer ter me ! I'll kill you if I kin git at yer. I will mun."

So Toby was reared in the midst of expletives and rocks. In these experiences he was far ahead of David who had Shimei to curse and throw stones at him on a single afternoon, while Toby had this kind of treatment every day. The boy may be said to have moved planet-like through a never-ending meteoric zone or belt, his own course being a most remarkable and erratic one, as he spent his life avoiding all bodies larger and heavier than himself.

In these flights, there was one line of Hamlet's soliloquy which could, very properly, have been quoted by the lad. He could truthfully have said :

"Toby, or not Toby, that is the question."

He fully realized that if one of the missiles flung at him should strike him, there would be no more Toby.

As for the "slings and arrows," Hamlet spoke about, he knew them not ; but the rocks and brick-bats were just as deadly. In the matter of "outra-geous fortune," he was once more in port, but adrift again in regard to "taking up arms against a sea of troubles." He preferred, in face of the peculiar difficulites of his life, to trust to his legs, leaving arms of all kinds out of the question.

Another surprising thing connected with these backyard eruptions was the speediness with which the whole affair would be forgotten by the chief actor. Perhaps not a half hour after, Matilda would be seen with the head of the offending child on her lap, while she, with motherly pride, would be seen combing out his kinks with a pair of cotton cards,

tying up his hair with gay-looking strings, or engaged in an exploration of the bushy head before
her, the nature of which investigation we beg to be
excused from mentioning.

There was still another feature of these affairs
which was the natural outcome of this treatment of
the boy. He came to wear a wary, anxious look
when approaching his mother, as if expecting
breakers ahead. Not knowing what he was to
receive, whether bread or a stone, when she cried
out: "Come hyer ter me!" he naturally drew
near with great misgivings and visible signs of
trepidation. It was noteworthy that Matilda spoke
just as sharply when she had food for him, as when
she had a cudgel hidden behind her with which to
dress him down. There were no visible signs by
which one could guess whether there was war or
peace in the air, but a most uncomfortable uncertainty hung over all. The boy had been deceived
many times in both ways; sometimes looking for a
beating, he received a piece of bread; and at other
times, going for one of the slim meals with which
his body and soul were kept together, suddenly,
without any warning, the stick would appear, the
rock would be lifted, Toby would scamper and then
would follow an excitement and commotion in the

backyard, which if projected on a commensurate scale among the nations, would be called a great war and require volumes to describe.

So Toby, not having a regular course of conduct on the part of his mother to go by, had to live moment by moment by faith, and sometimes with no faith at all, at least in the maternal head of the family. He had no chart or compass, and drifted never knowing where he was, nor when a rock would strike him and he be as effectually scuttled as any ship that ever sank. He trusted, in common parlance, to luck or, more truly speaking, to his eyes and heels; the one to discover the first signs of coming danger, the other to bear him away at race-horse speed.

To this day, we recall the cowed look of the boy, the anxious distrusting glance he would repeatedly cast at his mother from under his brows, while upon his lips would be seen the poorest attempt at a smile that one ever beheld. It was intended by him to be conciliatory and ingratiating, but often seemed to infuriate the strange, unnatural mother; and if she did happen to overflow in a Vesuvian way, it was simply amazing to watch the instantaneous disappearance of the smile, the equally quick gathering of a look of fear in his eyes,

while, with the absorbing purpose of immediate
escape in his mind, suddenly a pair of black soles
were turned motherward, and a pair of black legs
moved over the ground toward a place of safety with
a rapidity that would have made a castanet player
turn green with envy.

More than once I have seen him summoned
sharply by his mother to come before a group of
ladies and gentlemen standing on the gallery of
the "Big House." He would approach with his
half-imbecile manner, the watchful look in his
eye, and the painful attempt at a smile on his
mouth. Once I saw him, while waiting to be ad-
dressed, slowly raise one foot from the ground
and scratch a musquito from the calf of his left leg
with the toe of his right foot, without losing his
balance. Suddenly, Matilda turned like a cyclone
upon him and said:

"Whar's' yer perliteness? Why don't you
show yer mannus to de white folks?"

Down at once dropped Toby's foot from the
musquito hunt, the toes spoon-like scooped up and
threw backward some gravel, while his hand
pulled at a lock of hair in front. All of this was
intended for a bow, and was "sho'in his mannus."

It was pitiful to see the anxious, troubled look

cast out of the corner of his eye upon his mother, to see if his "mannus" had been acceptable.

Several times, we heard Mrs. Carleton say to Matilda:

"Why don't you put better clothes on your child?"

"Lor', Miss," replied the mother with a loud laugh, "dat boy wont keep nuffin' on, no matter what I puts on him. Ef I dress him in silk and satin, he wont have nuffin' 'tall to show fur it by night."

The idea of Toby being attired in silk and satin was decidedly mirth-provoking to Mrs. Carleton, but she did not smile; and, saying nothing more, went back into the house, though evidently not satisfied, while the boy under discussion was left to alternate between the trousers and shirt.

Sometimes we have heard an angry summons ring out on the air to him, and the order literally hurtled from the mouth:

"Go dis minute, you black imp you, an, rock yer Aunt Nancy's baby what's squallin' hitself ter death!"

Off went Toby like a shot, knowing well what the least delay would bring upon him and in a few moments a peculiar knocking sound on the cabin

floor would show that one of his daily duties had
been entered upon. The knocking was made by
the alternate rise and fall of a box without rockers
and which had the compliment conferred upon it
of being called a cradle. In this box was the yell-
ing young African he was commanded to quiet.
For some moments it would be doubtful which
would win the battle of competition of sound, the
cradle or the baby ; but Toby went at it systematic-
ally and doggedly ; he was used to noises and
especially this one, and so grasping the side of the
box in his hands, he met the duty of the hour,
which was to make that baby hush ; and this he did,
accomplishing the task in periods ranging from
five to twenty minutes. Little by little, the child
from being jerked about in the cradle, became
dizzy, then less vociferous, and finally was literally
banged and jarred into sleep or unconsciousness,
and the well-meaning nurse was free again.

Toby spent, as I have said, most of his life in
dodging rocks and brickbats. He had enough
thrown at him to have erected a monument of large
proportions.

The boy's life, was, in a sense, a military one,
full of sudden surprises by the foe and rapid retreats
on his part. It was in the line of falling back that

he attained such marvelous proficiency. From much experience, he became a perfect expert in bringing his own forces off the field, well-blown and exhausted, it is true, but always alive. Few military leaders have been able to do and that but rarely what Toby did in this regard most successfully for a number of years.

We can not but think that, if he had been placed at West Point, he would have developed into a master of strategy and swift retreat. Gen. Joseph E. Johnston, and Fabius, the famous Roman retreater might profitably sat at his feet had they only been his contemporaries. For all we know, a great military genius, a retreater, if not an advancer, passed away when Toby vanished from public view.

Several rumors of this colored family reached me after their emancipation and departure from the plantation. One was to the effect that Matilda had sickened and died. Here was another confirmation and proof of the wisdom in being able to conduct retreats. Just as Fabius, by his systematic and persistent fallings back, wore out opposing armies, so Toby, by skillful flights and rapid dodges and disappearances, kept himself alive, while his mother exhausted herself both in spirit and body by her frequent and protracted verbal and stone attacks and sank prematurely into the grave. She went down to the tomb, loaded with victories over her fugitive son, but they had been her own undoing. The inscription upon her sepulchre could very properly have been:

" WORN OUT IN RAISING TOBY. "

In other words, the human volcano reached the hour when it could do no more damage, its history ending with a little puff of breath from the open mouth, and lo! the explosions and stone projectiles of Matilda were over forever.

Poor little Toby! After the flight of busy years has crowded out many and important events, yet I can recall him as vividly as though it were but yesterday. Once more I see the woolly head, black face and half-clad form of the boy. I remember the anxious look, the apprehensive, apologetic smile, the suspicious attitude, and then, with the outbreak of hostilities, the sudden dash for life and liberty. I see the shirt streaming in a straight line, or the flapping, ill-fitting trousers held up with one hand, while the other hand digs into and saws the air most diligently, the feet pattering on the hard ground, the breath coming in peculiar

gasps through the set teeth ; and in another moment the flying vision flashes around the corner of
the smokehouse, and disappears in the garden
amid a shower of stones.

What became of Toby after the Emancipation,
is a mystery. There were two reports. One was
to the effect that, after his mother died, Toby fairly
languished. In spite of all her roughness, he
seemed to miss her as indeed he had every right
to do. He moped around in back alleys and
empty lots of the town, idly and disconsolately. He
lacked the inspiration of sudden movement, as of
yore ; there was no call for instantaneous and
violent exertion ; and so, Othello's occupation was
gone, and time hung heavy on the hands of the lad.

For awhile, he consorted with a crippled and
one-eared cur dog, which seemed as friendless,
hopeless and cast-off as himself. They were
often seen together in lanes, back alleys
and deserted outhouses, as if both avoided
recognition, and expected nothing and wanted
nothing save to be let alone. One day the
wheel of a great truck ran over the dog, and put
an end to his hot-water baths, and stick, rock and
hunger pangs, forever. After that, Toby was
again alone, now being observed, and now missed,

until one afternoon he was found dead in a stable loft.

Another report was that he lived to be fourteen or fifteen years of age, but always manifesting the greatest nervousness toward any missile flying through the air. He was often observed to give a brickbat lying in his path a wide berth in passing. Several times, he was seen looking at one, with an appearance of profound meditation. Doubtless, to his half-addled intellect, it was a thing of life, possessed inherent energy, and might any moment take wings and fly. As nearly all he had beheld prior to his mother's death were in the air, and moving in lines toward him he might have been pardoned for his exalted conception of that piece of matter, and his conclusion that none were to be trusted.

An ebony damsel of his age, taking a liking for the friendless boy, invited him to spend the evening at her father's house in the edge of the town. Near the house was a large brick-yard. It was not long before the watchful eye of Toby beheld the lofty stacks of red brick finished and ready for use, piles of broken ones in a corner, and a great kiln in full blast in the manufacture of thousands more. In less time than it takes to tell it, **Toby** had vanished. The yard, which **would** have been an ammunition depot for Matilda, and so a heaven to her, **was anything** but a paradise to Toby. Association **was** doubtless strong in him, and although the brick-thrower was in her grave, yet here were the bricks! And Fear cried out from within: "Let us be going! Why tarry we here **any** longer?"

After that, he was passing by a livery stable, when a horse gave a kick on the partition-wall close to him. It sounded like a brick striking a fence. Instantly, the old nature was in arms, or rather in feet, and the half-witted boy was seen flying like the wind for several blocks before he stopped to look back. The mother was dead, but her handiwork was still evident in the nervous system of the son. Her terror was still upon him, and that from a far distant world.

The second report went on to say that, one day, in running from some real or imaginary pursuer, Toby slipped on the ice-covered pavement as he turned a corner, and fell, striking his head against a large curbstone. He was picked up senseless and laid on some straw in the harness-room of a livery stable. He was aroused to a confused kind of consciousness in an hour or so, but looked ter-

rified as he heard the knocking and tramping of
the horses in their stalls, and tried to get up for
the old-time run ; but he was too weak and sank
back with an expression on his face of utter despair.

The owner of the stable, a white man, bent
over him and told him, in a kind voice, that nothing should hurt him. Whereupon, that curiously
blended look of anxiety, hope and dread stole into
the lad's face, and attempting to reach his front
lock of hair with his right hand, to "show his
mannus," the eyes of the boy suddenly glazed in
death and the tired, friendless soul left the half-
starved, emaciated body forever.

It was a deeply pathetic sight to see the ragged
figure on the straw pallet, the hand frozen in death
in the act of salutation, and the lines of a pitiful,
pleading expression still beheld in the sorrow and
pain-marked countenance.

The stable man, with his white and black host-
lers around him, looked silently at the dead form
of the boy, and then all walked out softly, with
that awe and melancholy upon the soul which is
always felt at the sight of an ended life, no matter
how young or how humble that life may have been.

Poor little Toby ! May he rest in peace ! This

world had for him a hard and bitter lot. He had but little pleasure in his brightest days, if any could have been called bright at all. Cuffs, kicks, upbraidings, chunks of wood, and stones, were the things which abounded in his life; and the aim and object of the boy was to miss as many of them as he could. His joy, if joy he had, was over such escapes.

We think of the One who said that not a sparrow falls to the ground without heavenly notice, and who spoke of a world where all tears are wiped away forever, and from off all faces.

We cannot but connect this Good Country with this hunted child, who never knew what a real home and true mother was; and the greater part of whose life was spent in running from flying missiles, amid heartless bursts of laughter from his own people. Stunted in growth and half-witted from cruel treatment he died early. I love to think of him as in "The Home-land," where the angels will be far kinder to him than were his own kindred and race, and where he will be better off in every way, and forever.